MYSTERY PLAYS
FOR
YOUNG ACTORS

by JOHN MURRAY

PLAYS, INC.
Publishers
Boston

Copyright © 1984
by John Murray

Reprinted   1989

Library of Congress Cataloging in Publication Data

Murray, John, 1923–
  Mystery plays for young actors.

  Contents: Airport adventure—Flight international—
Stage set for murder—[etc.]
    1. Detective and mystery plays, American.
  2. Children's plays, American.   [1. Mystery and detective plays.
    2. Plays]   I. Title.
PS3563.U77M9   1984   812'.54   84-11329
  ISBN 0-8238-0265-5 (pbk.)

Manufactured in the United States of America

Contents

OTHER BOOKS by

JOHN MURRAY

To the memory of
A. S. BURACK. . . .
my publisher, my teacher, my friend

Flight International

Characters

BRAD WINTERS
MARY THOMPSON
NEIL THORNE } *members of athletic team*
NANCY ADAMS
LYNNE NOLAN, *their coach*
TODD BAKER, *newspaper reporter*
SGT. RAY GRANGER
MR. KAUFMAN, *a jeweler*
DREW MANSFIELD
KAREN, *his wife*
HARVEY DAYTON, *a camera enthusiast*
MARIE, *his wife*
PORTER
POLICE OFFICER
AUNT MINERVA
ANNOUNCER, *offstage voice*
EXTRAS, *passengers and airline personnel*

TIME: *Evening; the present.*
SETTING: *The International Airport in a large city. Exits are right and left. Up right is another exit marked* GATES 32 TO 41. *Benches are located at angles facing audience, right and left. Information desk is up center. Various signs indicating airport facilities (*RESTAURANT, TELEPHONES, RESTROOMS, *etc.) are located right and left.* NOTE: *Male and female passengers and airline personnel appear throughout the play.*

AT RISE: ANNOUNCER's *voice is heard over offstage microphone.*
ANNOUNCER: Ladies and gentlemen, B.O.A.C. Flight No.
145 for London will depart in 40 minutes, from Gate 41.
(LYNNE, BRAD, MARY, NEIL, NANCY, *and* TODD *enter left,
carrying suitcases.* TODD *also carries a portable typewriter case.
They deposit suitcases near bench.* NANCY *is reading magazine
as she walks.)*
NANCY *(Looking up):* Miss Nolan, this article is great. *(Suddenly)* What's your sign, Miss Nolan?
LYNNE: Sign?
NANCY: Yes, zodiac sign. What's your birthday?
LYNNE: August 11.
NANCY: Leo—strong, determined, assertive, a great lover.
LYNNE *(Flustered):* Please, Nancy, there's no time for astrology now.
MARY: Nancy's always analyzing us, Miss Nolan. I'm a
Virgo—sensitive, creative.
NEIL: I'm an Aquarius, a born leader of business and
finance. *(Shrugs)* I can't even manage my monthly school
allowance.
NANCY: Go ahead and laugh, Neil. You can't deny your
destiny. *(Dramatically)* Our future is in the stars.
NEIL: And your head is in the clouds. (NANCY *makes a face,
sits on bench, continues to read.)*
MARY: I can't wait to get to England.
TODD: Same here. This is the biggest break of my newspaper career. *(Sheepishly)* Of course, I've been a reporter
for only six months, but this assignment to cover the
athletic competition, and a trip to England. Wow! *(He
taps his carrying case.)* This old typewriter will turn out
some great stories.
NANCY *(Looking up; suddenly):* Miss Nolan, something terrible is going to happen. I just know it! The signs are all
wrong.
LYNNE: Nancy, please. You're just upsetting everyone.
NANCY *(Defiantly):* I don't know why no one will listen to

me. *(To* NEIL*)* And I'm glad you're an Aquarius, Neil. You and I wouldn't make a good match at all.

NEIL: That's a relief! *(*TODD *puts down case, takes pad and pencil out of jacket pocket.)*

TODD: This will make a great human interest angle. *(He writes.)* "American athletes controlled by the stars." *(He returns pad and pencil to his pocket, picks up case.)* My editor will like that.

BRAD: Which newspaper do you work for, Todd?

TODD: The *Sun.* *(Jokingly)* Todd Baker's the name—news is my game! Who knows, my stories of the sports competition might even win an award. *(*BRAD *stares at* TODD, *turns.)*

BRAD: Miss Nolan, I have to make a telephone call.

LYNNE: O.K., but be sure to come back soon. We don't want to have to round up any strays when the plane leaves. *(*BRAD *exits.)*

NEIL *(Gesturing):* I don't know why, but I don't like that guy.

MARY: Brad? I think he's really cute.

NEIL *(Impatiently):* You would! What do we know about him? We never met him in any all-state competitions.

MARY: That's because he never competed in the United States. He originally came from Canada, and that's where he won the wrestling trophy.

NEIL *(Shaking his head):* Something about him bothers me. He doesn't seem real. And why did he have to make a telephone call?

NANCY: Maybe he wants to call his family.

TODD: Speaking of telephones, I'd better call the city desk with our flight schedule. Maybe they can arrange to have a photographer from the London office take some shots when we get there. *(He exits right.)*

NANCY: I'm thirsty. *(Looks at watch)* We still have time for a soda. *(To others)* Come on, kids—I'm buying.

LYNNE: Don't be long. We still have to check our luggage.

(NEIL, MARY and NANCY *exit left.* LYNNE *rearranges luggage.* RAY GRANGER, *a young man, and* MR. KAUFMAN, *a dignified, middle-aged gentleman, enter right.* KAUFMAN *carries a small, oblong box wrapped in cloth.* LYNNE *accidentally backs into* RAY. *She turns quickly.*) Oh, I'm terribly sorry. *(Surprised)* Say, haven't I met you somewhere?

RAY: Yes, of course! You're Lynne Nolan! *(Shakes her hand)* I'm Ray Granger. We met at your sister's.

LYNNE *(Nodding):* Sure. I remember. You're a police sergeant. It's nice to see you again. (RAY *gestures.*)

RAY: Lynne, I'd like you to meet Mr. Kaufman. *(Greetings are exchanged.)*

KAUFMAN: I represent the Metropolitan Gallery, and I'm going to England to exhibit the Titania emerald necklace. *(Taps box)*

RAY *(Cautiously):* Mr. Kaufman, not so loud. I wish you'd have listened to me and registered that necklace.

KAUFMAN: Nonsense! I've been taking care of myself—and my valuables—for thirty years. I wouldn't let this necklace out of my sight.

RAY *(Sighing):* I'll be glad when you're safely on the plane. (KAUFMAN *glances at his watch.*)

KAUFMAN: Perhaps I should call Mr. Simmons at the gallery and let him know I'm safe and sound.

RAY: I'll go with you.

KAUFMAN *(Emphatically):* That is unnecessary, Sergeant. You got me here safely. No one's going to rob me in the middle of a busy airport. I'll be right back. (KAUFMAN *exits right.* RAY *shakes his head.*)

LYNNE: Your job must be very exciting, Ray.

RAY: That's what everyone thinks, but it can be frustrating. I'm supposed to guard people like Mr. Kaufman, but they always want things their own way. *(Smiles)* But enough about me. What are you doing here? Are you going on a trip?

LYNNE *(Nodding):* Yes, we're going to the international

junior athletic competition in England—I'm the coach for the American team.

RAY: Great! (MARY, NEIL, *and* NANCY *re-enter.*)

LYNNE: Here are some of the team members now. (*To* MARY, NEIL *and* NANCY) Everybody, I'd like you to meet Sergeant Granger. (*Greetings are exchanged.*)

NANCY: Are you a policeman? (RAY *nods.*) Oh, I knew something exciting was going to happen tonight.

NEIL: Nancy is an astrology freak. She's always forecasting sinister happenings.

NANCY (*Ominously*): You'll find out how sinister *I* can be, Neil Thorne! (*To* RAY) Say, when is your birthday?

RAY: April 22nd.

NANCY: A Taurus! Liberal, assertive, capable of assuming command.

RAY: Thanks for the compliment, but I don't think our police captain agrees with you. (*They laugh.* BRAD *re-enters.*)

BRAD: The Canadian circuits were busy. I'll have to try again a little later.

TODD (*Re-entering*): Well, I got the city desk. The editor says he'll run a story on the team.

RAY (*Looking around*): Mr. Kaufman should be back by now.

BRAD: Who's Mr. Kaufman?

LYNNE (*Pointing to* RAY): Sergeant Granger is protecting him.

BRAD (*Interested*): Oh, really? How come?

RAY: He's carrying some valuable property.

TODD: Is that Kaufman of the Metropolitan Gallery?

RAY (*Skeptically*): Yes, but how did you know?

TODD (*Uneasily*): Well, uh—our paper is covering the London exhibit, and we found out that Kaufman is planning to exhibit the famous Titania emerald necklace.

RAY: Well, I hope the papers will hold the story until Kaufman arrives in London.

MARY: The necklace must be very valuable.

RAY: Let's just say that if I owned it, I could retire. (RAY *glances around nervously.* KAUFMAN *returns.*) Ah, there you are, Mr. Kaufman!

KAUFMAN (*To* RAY): Mr. Simmons is deeply grateful that you got me to the airport safely.

LYNNE: Mr. Kaufman, I'd like you to meet the members of our athletic team. (*Points to* BRAD) This is our wrestler. (*Points to* NEIL*)* Our star pole vaulter. (*Points to* MARY) Our gymnast. (*Points to* TODD) And this is a reporter for the *Sun,* who will cover the competition. I might add that he once was an archery champion.

KAUFMAN: Archery? Very interesting. I used to be a fair archer myself. (LYNNE *points to* NANCY.)

LYNNE: And this is our women's miler. She's also an ardent astrology buff.

KAUFMAN: Really? Why, astrology is my hobby, too. I'm a Capricorn. (*Smiles*) Well, this is quite a group. I'm sure you'll win many awards in the competition. (*Suddenly*) Oh, I completely forgot to tell Mr. Simmons something about the Guthrie exhibition that opens tomorrow. I must call him back at once.

BRAD: And I'd better try my Canadian call again. (KAUFMAN *and* BRAD *exit right.*)

LYNNE: I think we should check in our luggage.

TODD: I already sent mine through.

LYNNE (*Gesturing):* What about your typewriter? Aren't you going to check it?

TODD: No, I'll need it. I'm going to write my first article on the plane. (*Snaps fingers*) That reminds me. I have to pick up a copy of *Sports Illustrated.* They were supposed to run an article on the competition. I'll be right back. (*He exits right.*)

NEIL: Well, gang, let's take care of the luggage. (MARY, NEIL *and* NANCY *pick up suitcases.*)

RAY (*Picking up one of* LYNNE's *suitcases):* I'll give you a hand, Lynne.

LYNNE: Thanks, Ray. (RAY, LYNNE, MARY, NEIL *and* NANCY *exit left. In a moment,* DREW *and* KAREN MANSFIELD *enter right.* DREW *carries two suitcases, which he sets near bench, right.* KAREN *wears a corsage.*)

DREW *(Wiping his brow):* Whew! What an ordeal! Remind me never to get married again, Karen.

KAREN *(Feigning annoyance):* I resent that, Drew. *(Grins)* I was just beginning to like the idea.

DREW: Oh, you know what I mean, Karen. The ceremony—all those people—the flowers—*(Glances, around, smiles)* We're alone at last.

KAREN *(Looking at her ring):* Karen and Drew Mansfield! I still can't believe it!

DREW: And tomorrow we'll be in merry old England for two whole weeks! What a honeymoon we'll have—Trafalgar Square, the Changing of the Guard, the Tower of London . . .

KAREN: And don't forget the shops. We're going to buy all sorts of things.

DREW: Not so fast. Remember, we're on a very tight budget, in spite of that very generous cash gift from my Aunt Minerva.

KAREN *(Wryly):* She really enjoyed the wedding, didn't she?

DREW: I'm so happy she could be there. She flew all the way from Vancouver for the wedding, and tonight she's flying to Miami to board a ship for Venezuela. Imagine traveling so much!

KAREN *(Nodding):* She leads quite a life. She's probably at the other airport now. *(Quickly)* And we'd better make a last-minute check to see that everything is in order.

DREW: Why did I have to marry a systems analyst?

KAREN: Never mind. Do you have the airline tickets? (DREW *taps his lower left jacket pocket.*)

DREW: Check!

KAREN: The traveler's checks? (DREW *taps inner left jacket pocket.*)

DREW: Check!

KAREN: The hotel reservations? (DREW *taps inner right jacket pocket.*)

DREW: Check!

KAREN: Your passport?

DREW *(Pointing at luggage):* It's in my suitcase.

KAREN *(Shaking head):* Drew, you know you're always supposed to carry the passport with you. The customs inspector won't let you into England without it. (DREW *kneels, opens suitcase, frowns, holding up pink nightgown, a dress, high-heeled shoes, a wig, a make-up kit, and a purse.*)

DREW *(Upset):* Karen, something's wrong. I have the wrong suitcase. *(Takes passport from suitcase.)* Well, here's a passport. *(Opens passport, studies it)* It's Aunt Minerva's!

KAREN: Oh, no! She had all her luggage at the reception, so that she could go right to the airport afterward.

DREW: And she must have taken my suitcase by mistake. *(He glances at suitcase.)* Yes, it's almost exactly like mine.

KAREN *(Upset):* What are we going to do? Our plane leaves in a little while—and you have no passport.

DREW: Aunt Minerva will run into trouble without a passport, too. *(He stuffs clothing and passport into suitcase, closes it.)* I'd better call the hotel. Maybe Aunt Minerva hasn't left yet.

KAREN *(Near tears):* Oh, I hope you're right, Drew. Let's hurry! *(They pick up suitcases, exit right.* TODD *re-enters, carrying typewriter case. He glances around, impatiently.* BRAD *enters right.* TODD *is unaware of* BRAD, *but finally turns around and sees him.)*

TODD: Did your call go through?

BRAD *(Shaking his head):* No such luck. The Canadian circuits were still busy.

TODD: Where is everyone?

BRAD: I guess they're checking the luggage.

TODD: And I wonder what happened to Kaufman?

BRAD: He was in another telephone booth when I left him. Didn't you see him? You were making a call, too.

TODD *(Nodding):* I called my city editor.

BRAD *(Suspiciously):* Isn't it unusual for the *Sun* to send a reporter to cover a high school event?

TODD: No, everyone's interested in the international championships, Why, there might be a future Olympic champion in this group. By the way, I'm going to do a piece on your wrestling match.

BRAD: Is that so? *(Coldly)* Remind me to get a copy when it's published. (BRAD *looks at* TODD *suspiciously.*) Are you sure you're not here for another reason?

TODD *(Angrily):* I don't know what you're talking about. Look, Brad, you've acted strangely ever since I arrived. You keep following me around.

BRAD *(Ominously):* Maybe Nancy is right. Maybe something is going to happen tonight. *(Abruptly)* I think I'll go find Mr. Kaufman.

TODD *(Suspiciously):* Why are you so interested in him?

BRAD: He shouldn't be roaming around with a valuable necklace. *(Exits)*

TODD *(Thoughtfully):* Something might happen to him—or the necklace. *(Musing)* I think I'd better find Mr. Kaufman before Brad does. (TODD *exits right. In a moment,* DREW *and* KAREN, *carrying suitcases, enter right.*)

KAREN *(Upset):* Oh, now what are we going to do?

DREW *(Glumly):* I don't know. The people at the hotel said Aunt Minerva left about 45 minutes ago. Do you think we should try paging the other airport?

KAREN: But there isn't time! Our plane is due to leave in half an hour!

DREW: Do you think I can get through without a passport?

KAREN: I don't see how you can, and I won't go without you!

DREW *(Miserably):* But we planned this trip for so many months.

KAREN *(Soothingly):* Whatever we do, we'll do it together.

DREW *(Suddenly, smiling):* I have a great idea!

KAREN: What is it?

DREW: Aunt Minerva's make-up, her dress, her shoes, and her wig are in this suitcase. Best of all, I have her passport! People always said I resembled Aunt Minerva.

KAREN: It will never work!

DREW: Well, I've got to try it. *(Grabs her arm)* Come on! There's a restroom down the hall.

KAREN *(Impatiently)*: I just can't see—

DREW *(In falsetto voice)*: Come along, my child. You must never disobey your Aunt Minerva. *(They rush off right. HARVEY and MARIE DAYTON, a middle-aged couple, enter left. HARVEY carries a camera; camera case is slung over his shoulder. As they enter, HARVEY turns, focuses the camera on MARIE, gestures.)*

HARVEY: Say "Cheese," Marie. I want to get an action shot.

MARIE *(Angrily)*: Harvey Dayton! I've posed for a hundred pictures since you bought that silly camera!

HARVEY *(Offended)*: It's not a silly camera. It's a super-RX Panasonic Fujiyama micro-electric recorder with a 1.16 shutter speed and an integrated zoom lens.

MARIE: And you need a Ph.D. in engineering to operate the thing.

HARVEY: There's nothing to it. All you have to do is load the film, snap the shutter, and wait for the little beeping noise. When the flash goes off, you have a perfect picture.

MARIE *(Impatiently)*: Well, hurry up and take your shot! *(She smiles. HARVEY focuses camera, then frowns.)*

HARVEY *(Studying camera)*: It didn't beep!

MARIE: Maybe it's broken—*(Sarcastically)* I hope!

HARVEY *(Annoyed)*: I don't appreciate that, Marie. After all, this is our first trip abroad. I want to take pictures of the Coliseum, the Acropolis . . .

MARIE *(Sarcastically)*: We're going to London, Harvey. I think you should take a lesson in geography and forget that camera.

HARVEY *(Fussing with camera, then triumphantly)*: Ha! I see now what was wrong. I forgot to reload the camera with film. It'll take just a minute. *(Takes roll of film and instruction booklet from camera case)* The instructions are so easy to follow—this should be a snap. *(He steadies the camera and film as he reads.)* "Insert two silver-oxide batteries or one lithium battery into clip with the plus sign up." *(He shrugs.)* Oh, well, we'll forget the batteries. *(He continues to read.)* "Rotate film rewind crank (See diagram 2-A). Lift up and turn ASA/ISO film speed selector ring (See diagram 47-N)." I don't get it. *(Shakes his head and points at information desk up center)* Maybe that person at the information desk can help me.

MARIE *(Wearily):* I think that's above and beyond the airport's call of duty. (HARVEY *and* MARIE *walk to information desk.)*

HARVEY *(Continuing to read):* "Set shutter operation mode selector (See diagram 143-Y) to Auto—" (HARVEY *and* MARIE *pantomime conversation with clerk at information desk.* LYNNE, RAY, MARY, NEIL, *and* NANCY *re-enter right.)*

LYNNE: I wonder where Brad and Todd are. It's impossible to keep this group together. *(Sighs)* Thank goodness all our luggage is checked.

RAY: I'd better find Mr. Kaufman. (BRAD *re-enters right.)* Have you seen Mr. Kaufman?

BRAD: He was at the telephone booths. (TODD *re-enters right, carrying typewriter case.)*

NEIL: Did you get the magazine you wanted, Todd?

TODD: They were sold out of *Sports Illustrated.* (*To* BRAD) I didn't see you at the telephones.

BRAD *(Quickly):* I wanted to check the flight schedule. (MR. KAUFMAN *staggers in right. He clutches the opened box. He gropes for support, trips and almost falls, as* RAY *rushes forward and holds him up.)*

ALL *(Ad lib; alarmed):* Oh, no! Mr. Kaufman! What happened? *(Etc.)*

KAUFMAN *(Gasping):* The necklace—someone stole the

necklace! (*He drops empty box, which* LYNNE *picks up.* KAUF-
MAN *points at* NANCY.) It's—it's—the Ninth Sign.
NANCY *(Puzzled):* The Ninth Sign? (KAUFMAN *collapses to
floor.* RAY *kneels beside him, examines* KAUFMAN's *head.*)
RAY: Blood! Someone hit him—and hard. He's uncon-
scious. (PORTER *enters right.* RAY *calls to him.*) Porter, will
you help me get this man to your first-aid room? He's
been badly hurt.
PORTER: Yes, sir. (LYNNE *hands the empty box to* RAY, *who drops
it into his pocket.* RAY *and* PORTER *pick up* KAUFMAN, *exit
right.*)
LYNNE *(In disbelief):* I can't believe this is happening! *(To
others)* I hope we won't miss our plane. We might be
detained by the police.
NANCY *(Nodding):* That's true. We all knew Mr. Kaufman
was carrying the necklace.
TODD: Let's check with RAY. I don't want anything to happen to my first big assignment.
NEIL: Why don't we ask the sergeant if there's any way we
can help him out?
LYNNE: That's a good idea. (TODD, BRAD, LYNNE *and* NEIL
exit right.)
NANCY *(Frightened):* I knew something horrible was going
to happen. I just knew it!
MARY *(Sternly):* Will you forget your astrology? We have
enough trouble already. We're all under suspicion. Any
one of us might be accused of hitting Mr. Kaufman and
stealing the necklace.
NANCY *(Thoughtfully):* What could he have meant by the
Ninth Sign? *(Suddenly)* The Ninth Sign of the zodiac! Of
course! Mr. Kaufman said astrology was his hobby! He
must have been trying to tell us something about his
attacker.
MARY: If Mr. Kaufman recognized the thief, why didn't he
mention his name?
NANCY: I can't answer that. *(Thoughtfully)* Let's see—Miss

Nolan is a Leo. You're a Virgo. Neil is an Aquarius, and I'm a Gemini.

MARY: And what about Brad and Todd?

NANCY: Brad's a Scorpio. And Todd is a Libra. That was the first thing that I asked him when we met tonight. So I don't know what Mr. Kaufman meant by the Ninth Sign. None of us was born under the Ninth Sign.

MARY: What about Sergeant Granger? Didn't you say he was a Taurus?

NANCY: He's not a suspect! He was guarding Mr. Kaufman.

MARY: He didn't do a very good job.

NANCY: That's unfair. Mr. Kaufman insisted on going off alone to the telephone. Besides, Taurus isn't the Ninth Sign.

MARY: I guess you're right. *(She glances around.)* There are plenty of signs in here. Information—restaurant— telephone booths. Maybe he wasn't referring to the zodiac.

NANCY: I don't know what he meant.

ANNOUNCER *(Over offstage mike):* B.O.A.C. Flight No. 145 for London, England, will board at Gate 41 in 15 minutes. All passengers are requested to go to the gate at once. Thank you.

MARY: We're going to miss our plane! We'd better find the others. *(They exit right.* HARVEY *and* MARIE DAYTON *leave information desk, walk down center.)*

HARVEY: That clerk wasn't much help. I still don't know how to insert the film into any of the take-up spools or move the six slots. *(Thrusts the manual into the carrying case)* I don't understand why I can't make the thing work.

MARIE: You even have trouble at home with an electric toothbrush.

HARVEY: Please, Marie, you're no help at all. *(Suddenly)* I know! I'll call Roscoe! He knows all about cameras.

MARIE *(With resignation):* Go ahead. That brother of yours should be good for something. *(They exit left.* KAREN *re-enters right, carrying suitcase, and walks center.)*

KAREN *(Calling off):* Well, come on, Drew. This was your idea, remember? (DREW *enters timidly. He wears a dress, wig, and high-heeled shoes. He clutches suitcase and purse. He wobbles uncertainly on the shoes as he joins* KAREN.)

DREW *(Nervously):* How do I look? Do you think I'll pass as Aunt Minerva when we have to show our passports?

KAREN: Not unless you do something about your walk. You swagger like a tackle for the New York Jets.

DREW *(Weakly):* Thanks for the encouragement. *(He touches his face.)* I wish I had sunglasses. *(Determined)* Karen, we're going on this honeymoon, no matter what.

KAREN: The authorities are probably watching us now. They have TV cameras all over this place. *(She stifles a laugh.)*

DREW *(Between clenched teeth):* Please stop laughing at me.

KAREN *(Soberly):* I'm sorry, Drew.

DREW: Please call me Aunt Minerva.

KAREN: I still think we should spend our honeymoon in the States.

DREW *(Firmly):* Karen, we're spending it in England! That is, if my make-up holds up. *(Suddenly)* The make-up! I left it in the restroom. (DREW *tugs at* KAREN's *arm.*) We have to get it.

KAREN: Please forget the make-up.

DREW *(Affectedly):* Why, I'd look a perfect fright in the morning without my make-up!

KAREN *(Chuckling):* Oh, Drew! *(They exit right. In a moment,* RAY, LYNNE, BRAD, NANCY, MARY, NEIL *and* TODD *re-enter.)*

RAY *(Sighing):* Well, the ambulance took Kaufman to the hospital. He still hasn't regained consciousness.

LYNNE: I hope he'll be all right.

RAY: I called the police station, and they're sending someone right out. *(Pats his coat pocket)* Thanks for giving me
the jewel box, Lynne. We'll try to raise some fingerprints
at headquarters.

BRAD: Fingerprints? I never thought of that.

TODD: The thief might have worn gloves. I'm sure he's too
clever to have left fingerprints on the box.

RAY *(Upset):* I never should have left Kaufman alone—
even for a minute!

MARY: But you did your job, Sergeant—you got him to the
airport safely.

TODD *(To RAY):* What are you going to do next? It isn't
possible to search the passengers on all the flights scheduled for departure.

RAY *(Nodding):* That *would* be a tall order. There are eight
flights scheduled in the next hour. And the thief has
probably left the airport already.

MARY: Maybe he had a partner. He could have passed the
necklace on to someone else—someone who's miles
away by now.

NANCY *(Solemnly):* I still think astrology is the key to the
problem.

RAY: Mr. Kaufman did say something about a sign before
he passed out, didn't he?

NANCY *(Nodding):* Yes. The Ninth Sign. But none of us was
born under the Ninth Sign.

NEIL: Mr. Kaufman wouldn't have known our birthdays,
anyway.

TODD: Of course not. We just met him.

RAY: I like the theory about a confederate. If the thief
boarded the plane with the necklace, his things would be
searched at customs. He had to dispose of the necklace
before take-off.

BRAD: That's right.

NANCY *(Musing):* The Ninth Sign—*(She flips through the*

magazine, reads.) "November 22 to December 21." *(She
closes the magazine, sighs.)* I don't see any clue there. *(Desperately)* But it must mean something. (TODD *rubs his
head, staggers.* RAY *grabs his arm, steadies him.)*
LYNNE: Todd—what's the matter?
TODD *(Unsteadily):* I don't know. I don't feel very well. All
this excitement—my first assignment.
RAY: Maybe we'd better get you to the first aid station.
(TODD *nods.)*
TODD: I think that's a good idea.
RAY: I'll come with you.
TODD: I can get there myself.
BRAD: You really shouldn't go alone.
TODD *(Insistently):* I'm all right, I tell you. I just need a little
air.
LYNNE: I think we should all stay together.
MARY: Yes, Todd, we're all going with you.
RAY *(Nodding):* That's a good idea. There's a person loose
who will stop at nothing.
BRAD: I'm going to try that phone call one more time.
(RAY, LYNNE, MARY, NEIL, NANCY, BRAD *and* TODD *exit
right.* HARVEY *and* MARIE *enter left. They sit on bench, left.)*
HARVEY *(Fussing with camera):* Good old Roscoe! I knew
he'd be able to tell me how to load this camera.
MARIE: You haven't done it yet.
HARVEY: It's as good as done, Marie. *(He fumbles with the
camera, inserts new roll of film.)* This film doesn't seem to
fit. *(Accusingly)* Marie, you bought the wrong size film.
MARIE *(Sighing):* Harvey, why don't you just put the camera away?
HARVEY: You're just afraid to face a challenge.
MARIE *(Glumly):* I married you, didn't I? (HARVEY *sputters,
pounds film into camera, snaps it shut.)*
HARVEY: There! The film is in! *(He gestures.)* Please stand
up, Marie. *(She complies.)* I'd like a nice pose. Say

"Cheese." (MARIE *smiles.* HARVEY *stands, presses button, stares at camera, and pounds on the release button. Upset*) It didn't beep!

MARIE: Good. Now I won't have to pose for any more stupid pictures.

HARVEY *(Loudly):* It's going to beep or I'm going to bop someone! (HARVEY *and* MARIE *sit on bench, examine camera in pantomime.* DREW, *still in women's clothing and carrying suitcase and purse, enters right, followed by* KAREN, *who carries suitcase.*)

KAREN: I know you'll never get away with this crazy scheme, but that's what I like about you. *(She smiles.)* Life will never be dull with you around.

DREW: How about a kiss for your dear, old Aunt Minerva?

KAREN *(Laughing):* I wouldn't dream of smudging your make-up. *(They continue to talk in pantomime.* RAY, LYNNE, TODD, MARY, NEIL *and* NANCY *re-enter.* TODD *is agitated.*)

TODD: I'm telling you, there's nothing wrong with me. *(He glances around nervously, grips the typewriter case.)*

MARY: We'd better board the plane. It's almost flight time.

NEIL: Brad isn't back yet. I never trusted that guy. Maybe he stole the necklace.

LYNNE: What a terrible thing to say!

RAY: Look—we can't start accusing each other. *(He shakes his head.)* If Mr. Kaufman recognized his assailant, why didn't he name him? There's something wrong— something we're missing.

NANCY *(Excitedly):* I think I've figured it out! Mr. Kaufman couldn't name his attacker because he didn't know his name! Miss Nolan, don't you remember? When you introduced him to us, you didn't mention our names.

LYNNE *(Recollecting):* You're right—I didn't.

NANNY: You referred to our sports.

RAY *(Slowly):* A wrestler, a pole vaulter, a gymnast, a mile runner. *(Nods)* That would be the only identification that Kaufman could make.

TODD *(Relieved):* Well, that lets me out. I'm not a member of the team.

NANCY *(Warily):* No, but you mentioned that you had won school awards for archery. Each zodiac sign is identified by a special character. Aries is the Ram; Taurus, the Bull; Capricorn, half goat, half fish. Mr. Kaufman knew that "The Ninth Sign" was the only way he could name his assailant!

NEIL: I get it! The Ninth Sign had to refer to a particular sporting event. (NANCY *opens the magazine.*)

NANCY: Here! *(She reads. At the same time, BRAD enters right. He stands aside from group, observes the action.)* "The Ninth Sign—Sagittarius. A Centaur drawing a bow and arrow—the Archer!" *(Everyone looks suspiciously at TODD, as DREW and KAREN leave the bench, and prepare to exit through loading gate exit. They pass the group as HARVEY and MARIE approach. HARVEY focuses camera at MARIE. NANCY points at TODD.)* It was you, Todd. You attacked Mr. Kaufman and stole the necklace! You're the Archer!

TODD: You don't know what you're talking about. (BRAD *steps forward, grabs TODD's arm.*)

BRAD: She's right. (TODD *breaks BRAD's grip, spins around.*) You see, I called the *Sun* a little while ago, but I couldn't speak to the editor. When I called back again just now, I got the city desk.

TODD *(Shakily):* You called the *Sun?*

BRAD: The paper didn't send a reporter to cover the London competition. The editor never heard of you. You're an impostor!

NANCY *(To TODD):* Also a thief. You probably had a confederate, but you never had the chance to pass the necklace to him. And—you refused to check your typewriter. Why was it so important to keep it with you?

RAY: Let me see that case, Todd. (TODD *protests, but* RAY *grabs it, opens it, and pulls out necklace.*)
MARY: The necklace!
OTHERS *(Ad lib):* Oh, no! Todd's the thief. Look at that! *(Etc.)*
RAY: I think this is sufficient evidence. *(He puts necklace into his pocket, sets down typewriter case.)*
TODD: All right! I knew about the London exhibit. I was told that Kaufman would board a plane tonight with the necklace. *(To* LYNN) I joined the group so that I'd have a chance to steal it without being suspected. *(Laughs hoarsely)* Yes, I had a partner who would take the necklace, and then I would disappear before take-off. A perfect setup! And you're not going to stop me now! *(Quickly, he draws a gun from his pocket, waves it viciously.* TODD *turns, grabs* DREW, *who is passing.* KAREN *screams as* TODD *encircles* DREW's *neck with his free arm.)* If anyone tries to stop me, I'll kill this woman. (HARVEY, *concentrating on taking* MARIE's *picture, steps in front of* TODD. *Camera flash goes off with loud beep, the bright light momentarily blinds* TODD, *and he releases* DREW. DREW's *wig falls off in the scuffle.* DREW *clouts* TODD *with his purse.* TODD *staggers as* RAY *grabs his gun.* POLICE OFFICER *rushes in, right.)*
RAY: Officer, take this man to headquarters. I'll be down shortly to file a report.
POLICE OFFICER: Yes, Sergeant Granger. (POLICE OFFICER *grabs* TODD's *arm, leads him off, right.* RAY *turns to* DREW.)
Ray: I hope you're not hurt, ma'am. (RAY *looks at the wig on the floor, stares at* DREW, *does a double-take.)*
DREW *(Indignantly):* I'm no lady!
KAREN *(Rushing to* DREW): Oh, Drew! I'm so glad you're all right! *(Seeing* RAY's *puzzled look; to* RAY) You see, my husband lost his passport, and he dressed as his Aunt Minerva, and—oh, what's the use?

RAY *(Dazed):* No need to explain. *(To* HARVEY*)* And I want to thank you, sir. That camera flash was a life saver.

MARY: Harvey, I'm so proud of you.

HARVEY: There's nothing like a Fujiyama. *(He beams.)* Yes, sir! When Harvey Dayton beeps, he really beeps! (HAR-VEY *and* MARIE *exit through gate, up right.* AUNT MINERVA, *carrying a suitcase, enters right.)*

AUNT MINERVA *(Calling):* Oh, Karen! There you are!

KAREN *(Surprised):* Aunt Minerva! Are we glad to see you!

AUNT MINERVA *(Joining the group):* I took Drew's suitcase by mistake. *(She displays the suitcase.)* When I looked for my make-up, I realized what a terrible thing I'd done. *(She glances around.)* But where is the dear boy?

DREW *(Sheepishly):* Hello, Aunt Minerva. (AUNT MINERVA *gasps when she recognizes* DREW. *She picks ups the wig, clucks disapproval.)*

AUNT MINERVA: My best dress and my favorite wig! Oh, Drew!

KAREN: We'll explain everything later. (DREW *puts* AUNT MINERVA'*s suitcase near her, takes his.)*

DREW: I'll return your dress and—er—other things when we get back to the States, Aunt Minerva. We have to rush to make our plane. (KAREN *takes* DREW'*s arm.)*

KAREN: Drew, we're really going on a honeymoon! 'Bye, Aunt Minerva! *(They exit.)*

AUNT MINERVA *(Smiling, embarrassed):* Drew is really a nice boy, when you get to know him. But he does have an odd sense of humor sometimes. *(Shakes her head, exits right)*

LYNNE *(Shaking head):* This has been some night!

NEIL *(To* BRAD): I owe you an apology, Brad. I thought—

BRAD *(Raising hand):* Forget it.

MARY *(To* BRAD): Brad, by calling the *Sun* to check on Todd's credentials, you saved the day.

LYNNE *(Suddenly):* We'd better board the plane. *(To* RAY) Are we free to leave?

RAY *(Nodding):* Yes, I think I can clear everything up at the station.

NANCY: And I'm going to check our horoscopes for tomorrow. *(She waves the magazine.)*

ALL *(Together):* No astrology, please!

NANCY *(Happily):* We're going to win the competition. It's in the stars! (RAY *waves as the group exits. Curtain*)

THE END

Production Notes

FLIGHT INTERNATIONAL

Characters: 7 male; 6 female; 3 male or female for Porter, Announcer and Police Officer; as many male and female extras as desired for passengers and airline personnel.

Playing Time: 35 minutes.

Costumes: Suitable travel attire for all principals. Drew changes into dress, wig, and high-heeled shoes, and carries a purse. Police Officer wears uniform. Karen wears corsage, ring. Airline personnel wear suitable uniforms.

Properties: Several suitcases, one containing dress, wig, shoes, passport, make-up; purse; typewriter case containing necklace; oblong box with cloth; magazine; camera; camera case, instruction booklet and film; pencil and pad; prop gun.

Setting: International Airport in a large city. Exits are right and left. Up right is exit marked GATES 32 TO 41. Benches are located right and left, at an angle, facing audience. Information desk is up center. Signs indicating RESTAURANT, TELEPHONE, RESTROOMS, NEWSPAPERS AND BOOKS are right and left. General activity of passengers and airline personnel should occur throughout the play.

Sound: Offstage flight announcements, as indicated.

The Looking Glass Murder

Characters

SALLY, *20*
TESS, *her friend*
MOM, *her mother*
PATTY, *12, her sister*
FRANK ⎫
LEFTY ⎪
MRS. MURPHY ⎬ *Mom's boarders*
MRS. STEVENS ⎪
MR. BLY ⎭
TIM, *a police officer*

SETTING: *Rooftop of an apartment house. Upstage there is a brick parapet about three feet high, which runs entire length of stage. In center of parapet is fire escape railing, leading to lower floors. Roof door is at right.*

AT RISE: SALLY *and* TESS *stand at parapet, talking quietly.* MRS. MURPHY *and* MRS. STEVENS *sit down center, shelling peas into pan.*

MRS. MURPHY: A person isn't safe in this neighborhood any more.

MRS. STEVENS: Poor old Mrs. Frazier! I wonder how much money was hidden in her room when she was murdered.

MRS. MURPHY: We'll never know exactly, Mrs. Stevens, but I'm sure it was a fortune. She was a real recluse. Imagine having all that money and living in this place! *(Shakes her head)* You never can tell about some people.

MRS. STEVENS: The worst part is that her killer got away. The police don't have a clue. *(They continue to shell peas, as* SALLY *and* TESS *cross down right.)*

TESS: You can eat at my place if you like, Sally.

SALLY: Thanks, Tess. I'm not hungry. I'm so worried about Frank.

TESS *(Helpfully):* Try not to worry. The police will find him.

SALLY *(Frightened):* I don't want them to find him! *(Slowly)* You don't think he had anything to do with Mrs. Frazier's death, do you?

TESS *(Awkwardly):* Honestly, I don't know. (MRS. MURPHY *and* MRS. STEVENS *stop talking and listen.)*

SALLY *(Defiantly):* Well, *I* know. Frank didn't kill Mrs. Frazier. She was his friend. He always helped her.

MRS. MURPHY *(Speaking up):* Helped? That terrible young man went to Mrs. Frazier's apartment just to find where she kept her money.

SALLY *(Angrily):* That's not true, Mrs. Murphy!

MRS. STEVENS *(Quickly):* Why did Frank run away, then?

SALLY *(Tearfully):* I don't know, but I'm sure he's innocent. And it's awful the way everyone is talking about him!

MRS. MURPHY *(Standing):* If you're not the limit, Sally! I saw Frank with my own eyes, coming out of Mrs. Frazier's apartment. *(She nods emphatically.)* They found poor old Mrs. Frazier's body only a short time later.

SALLY: You might have been mistaken.

MRS. MURPHY: The police didn't think so. They'll find him, all right! *(To* MRS. STEVENS) Come along, we'd better get down to our apartments. *(She glares at* SALLY.) The murderer might come back! (MRS. STEVENS *stands, gathers pan and bag of peas and walks out door right.* MRS. MURPHY *follows her off.)*

TESS: Don't listen to her, Sally. She's just an old gossip.

SALLY *(Dejectedly):* I wish Frank hadn't run away. It looks so bad for him! You heard Mrs. Murphy. She told the police that she saw him leaving Mrs. Frazier's place last night.

TESS: You said Frank often went there to help her.

SALLY: That's right, but, someone else must have gone there after Frank left. Frank is innocent!

TESS *(Putting arm around* SALLY'*s shoulder):* I never knew you cared so much about Frank.

SALLY *(Sitting):* He's just wonderful. Frank and Lefty have been our dearest friends since Dad died. We used to come up here to the roof, and Frank would read to me. Does that sound silly?

TESS: No, not at all. *(Sits)*

SALLY *(Smiling):* Do you know, Tess, Frank introduced me to my favorite books—*Alice and Wonderland* and *Through the Looking Glass.* I never think of them as children's books. I love the Mad Hatter, the March Hare—why, Frank would even pretend to be the King. He liked to look at the city lights and tell me that this was his kingdom.

TESS *(Musing): Alice in Wonderland.*

SALLY: The roof of this building *was* a wonderland! *(She sobs.)* And now he's gone.

TESS *(Awkwardly):* Please don't cry. Someone will clear his name. *(She glances at wristwatch.)* Why, it's almost six o'clock. I'd better get home. *(Standing, puts hand on* SALLY'*s shoulder)* Maybe I'll see you later.

SALLY: Perhaps. I'd like to stay here for a while. *(She attempts a smile.)*

TESS: Goodbye. *(She walks right.)*

SALLY: Goodbye, Tess. Thanks for everything. (TESS *exits.* SALLY *stands and walks to parapet. She stares out over it.* MOM *enters right with* TIM, *a police officer.)*

MOM: I thought we'd find you here, Sally.

SALLY *(Turning):* Hello, Mom. Hi, Tim.

TIM: Hi, Sally. I want to ask you a few questions about Frank.

SALLY *(Anxiously):* Have you found him?

TIM: Not yet. We've put an all-points bulletin out for him.

MOM: Poor Frank!

TIM *(Defensively):* He ran away, didn't he?

SALLY: What else could he do? Mrs. Murphy went screaming to the police that Frank had killed Mrs. Frazier. No one would give him a chance to explain.

TIM: Running away never helped anyone. *(He takes notebook and pencil from his pocket.)* Frank's been boarding with your family about five years, right?

SALLY: Yes.

MOM: After my husband's death, I had to do something to make ends meet, so I advertised for boarders.

TIM: And Frank and Lefty answered your ad. (MOM *nods.* TIM *turns to* SALLY.) Did Frank ever talk about his background?

SALLY: No, he didn't talk about himself much. I don't think he had any family.

TIM: How about friends? Did he have any in the city?

SALLY: I never met them. Of course, he knew the people at the plant where he worked.

TIM: How did he meet Mrs. Frazier?

SALLY: One day Frank happened to see her in her backyard, and they began to talk. Then he started doing little chores for her around her place. She seemed fond of him.

TIM *(Quickly):* Did you know that Mrs. Frazier had a lot of money?

SALLY: There are always stories about rich old recluses, but she lived simply.

TIM: She had some valuable jewelry. I questioned the tenants, and they're willing to swear to that.

SALLY: I heard she had some, but I never saw it.

TIM: Did you ever see her wearing a string of pearls?

MOM: I saw them! She invited me in for a cup of tea one day, and I remember she wore a string of pearls!

TIM: Did Frank ever see the pearls?

MOM *(Thoughtfully):* I can't be sure. . . . *(Suddenly)* Why, yes! He came in that day while I was there to try to fix Mrs. Frazier's stove. He must have seen them.

SALLY *(Agitatedly):* That doesn't prove he killed her, Mom. Why are you asking us these questions, Tim?

TIM: I just want to get all the facts. We have Mrs. Murphy's testimony that he left Mrs. Frazier's place early last evening. She recognized his checkered sport coat. A little while later we got an anonymous call that Mrs. Frazier had been murdered, shot.

MOM: Tell me, Tim, are the pearls gone?

TIM *(Nodding):* They must have been taken by the murderer. Most folks believed that Mrs. Frazier had a large sum of money hidden in her apartment, but we didn't find that, either.

SALLY: I know you have your job to do, Tim, but *(Imploringly)* you must help me clear Frank's name.

TIM: That's a tough assignment, considering he's been missing since the murder.

SALLY: Aren't there any other suspects?

TIM: Not yet.

SALLY *(Quickly):* Did you question Mr. Bly?

TIM: Bly? Oh, he's the strange man in the rear apartment. I did talk to him, but I couldn't tie him with Mrs. Frazier. I think he's mad as a hatter.

SALLY *(Musing):* The Mad Hatter! Why, that's like *Alice in Wonderland.* *(Suddenly)* Did you find the gun?

TIM: No, the murderer must have taken it with him.

SALLY: Frank never owned a gun.

TIM: I'd like to see Frank's room again. Maybe we'll find a clue to where he's hiding.

MOM *(To* SALLY*):* Come along, Sally. We have to eat dinner. Patty must be home by now.

SALLY *(Sighing):* All right, Mom. (TIM, MOM, *and* SALLY *exit.* PATTY, *a little girl, steps from behind opened roof door where she has been hiding. She walks to parapet, peers at section of building across courtyard. She raises her right hand as though she is holding gun, and levels it forward. She shakes her head.* LEFTY *enters silently. He watches* PATTY. *Cautiously, he tiptoes behind her, grabs her by the shoulders, spins her around. She screams.*)

PATTY: Lefty! You scared me!

LEFTY: Mom's looking for you, Patty. Where have you been?

PATTY: Up here.

LEFTY: Mom just left the roof. She didn't see you. Were you hiding?

PATTY *(Slowly):* Yes. *(Points)* Behind this door.

LEFTY: Then I suppose you heard that police officer talking to Sally. *(She tries to pull away.)*

PATTY: Let me go! You're hurting me—I'm going to tell Mom.

LEFTY *(Releasing* PATTY): Don't go yet. I think you know something about Mrs. Frazier's murder.

PATTY: What do you mean?

LEFTY: You were up on the roof about the time she was killed last night.

PATTY *(Frightened):* How did you know?

LEFTY: It was a guess, but it seems I was right. You're always up here. What did you see?

PATTY *(Defiantly):* I didn't see anything.

LEFTY: I think you know something. You wouldn't want me to tell Tim, would you?

PATTY: Oh, no!

LEFTY: I've been watching you all day. You're frightened. You hardly touched your breakfast. *(Angrily)* Now, what did you see last night? *(He swings her roughly around to parapet edge, and points down.)* What did you see down there? (SALLY *enters unnoticed. She quickly steps behind roof door.*)

PATTY *(Hysterically):* I saw him kill her! I saw him shoot

Mrs. Frazier! (*She pulls away from* LEFTY.) Oh, Lefty, don't tell Mom or Tim.

LEFTY (*Coldly*): Just tell me what you saw.

PATTY (*Frightened, quickly*): I saw Mrs. Frazier standing by her bedroom window. Then I saw a hand holding a gun. (PATTY *raises her right hand as though holding gun.*) Mrs. Frazier tried to back away, but then she fell to the floor. I didn't hear the gun go off. It must have been one of the silent kind.

LEFTY: What else did you see?

PATTY: A man went to the dresser and took something out of the top drawer. He put it into his pocket and left.

LEFTY (*Quickly*): Who was the man?

PATTY: I couldn't see his face. I only saw his coat—a checkered sport coat, just like Frank's! (*She starts to cry.* SALLY *steps forward quickly.*)

SALLY: Patty! Why didn't you tell me about Frank?

PATTY (*Surprised*): Sally! I didn't want you to worry.

SALLY: You poor dear! (*Firmly*) We have to tell Tim everything. Maybe someone else wore Frank's jacket. It's missing now. (*Thinking, looks around*) Patty, where were you standing last night?

PATTY (*Going to parapet and pointing*): Right here. The shade was up in Mrs. Frazier's bedroom, and I looked through the window. (SALLY *looks over parapet.*)

SALLY: But that's impossible!

LEFTY: Why? What do you mean?

SALLY: Patty couldn't have seen into Mrs. Frazier's room. Her apartment is directly under this roof! And Patty pointed across the court!

LEFTY: That doesn't make sense.

PATTY: I saw it, I tell you! (*She points across and down.*) There's the window. You can see Mrs. Frazier's bedroom. There! That's how I saw it last night. (LEFTY *and* SALLY *look over parapet.*)

SALLY *(Puzzled):* But that's not Mrs. Frazier's apartment.

LEFTY *(Slowly):* Wait a minute! It looks like Mrs. Frazier's bedroom. There's her dresser and the chair, and some old hat boxes on the bed.

SALLY *(Suddenly):* It's a mirror! It's a reflection in a looking glass!

LEFTY *(Excitedly):* You're right. We can see the reflection of Mrs. Frazier's bedroom in the mirror.

SALLY *(Thoughtfully):* A looking glass—

LEFTY *(Whistling softly):* And Patty saw the murder through a reflection in the mirror.

PATTY: I told you what I saw. I don't know about any mirror.

SALLY: We'd better get Tim. (MR. BLY *enters.*)

BLY: May I join you?

LEFTY *(Startled):* Mr. Bly!

BLY *(Gesturing at* SALLY): I'd like to talk to the young lady.

SALLY: I was just about to leave.

BLY *(Smiling):* No one wishes to remain alone after a murder.

LEFTY: What do you know about it?

BLY *(Coolly):* Nothing, really. Murder isn't to my taste at all. *(He sighs.)* Oh, well.

LEFTY *(Suddenly):* Do you own a checkered jacket?

BLY: A checkered jacket? *(He laughs.)* Now, do I look the type?

LEFTY: No, I guess not. *(To* SALLY) We'd better get down for dinner.

SALLY *(Suddenly):* No, I want to stay here, after all. I have to think things out. I'm not afraid.

BLY: A very brave young lady. I understand that your boarder—Frank—is wanted for the murder.

SALLY *(Sharply):* No, he's not. The police want him for questioning, that's all.

BLY: Is there really any difference? *(He walks right, turns and faces* SALLY.) I'll see you later. I shall go to the corner for the evening paper. *(Exits)*

PATTY: He's strange! I don't like him.

SALLY *(Musing):* He had such a funny smile on his face, as though he knew something. The Mad Hatter—this whole thing is like *Alice in Wonderland!*

LEFTY *(Scornfully):* Now I've heard everything!

SALLY: No, Lefty, I know I'm on to something. *(As if thinking aloud)* Mrs. Frazier might have been the Queen of Hearts. And the Mad Hatter—and the murder in the looking glass. *Through the Looking Glass!*

LEFTY: And the Knave of Hearts ran away with the Queen's pastry. Only we're looking for a string of pearls, not tarts.

SALLY *(Musing):* I wonder what Alice actually saw in the looking glass. *(Quickly)* Lefty, please take Patty down to dinner.

LEFTY: O.K., but don't stay up here too long. (LEFTY *and* PATTY *exit.* SALLY *sits on parapet, covers her face with her hands.* FRANK, *wearing checkered sport coat and looking tired and disheveled, climbs up fire escape center and drops onto roof.* SALLY, *startled, jumps up, rushes into his arms.*)

SALLY *(Half crying):* Oh, Frank! Where have you been? Everyone is looking for you.

FRANK *(Urgently):* I was a fool to run away, but I didn't know what to do.

SALLY: Frank, did you—oh, please tell me the truth. (FRANK *steps back.*)

FRANK *(Upset):* You don't think I killed Mrs. Frazier, do you?

SALLY: Of course I don't, but everybody is accusing you.

FRANK: I thought you trusted me.

SALLY: I do trust you, Frank, and I'll help you. I'll do anything—but I must know the truth.

FRANK *(Upset):* This is all a nightmare. *(Resolutely)* I want to see Tim. *(He reaches into pocket and draws out string of pearls.* SALLY *stares at it.)*

SALLY *(Nervously):* Where did you get those pearls?

FRANK: I found them in my jacket pocket last night.

SALLY: But how did they get there? Who could have put them there?

FRANK: If I knew that, we'd have the murderer.

SALLY: Where have you been hiding all day?

FRANK: In the deserted warehouse down the block.

SALLY: Please tell me what happened last night.

FRANK: I went to Mrs. Frazier's after supper, and she wanted me to go to the store. I bought the groceries, and on my way back to her apartment with them, I stopped off in my room for a minute to pick up this jacket. *(Thoughtfully)* It's odd, now that I think of it.

SALLY: What's odd?

FRANK: I always hang the jacket in my closet, but I found it thrown across the foot of the bed.

SALLY *(Slowly):* So you were wearing that jacket when you went back to Mrs. Frazier's the second time.

FRANK: Yes, I put it on and went to Mrs. Frazier's apartment with the groceries. When I went in *(Pauses)*—you know what I found.

SALLY: You mean she was dead when you found her?

FRANK *(Nodding):* Yes. I know it looks bad for me, but that's the truth.

SALLY: I believe you, Frank. We'll have to convince the police, that's all. *(Pauses)* I have a question, Frank. It sounds silly, but it could be terribly important. Where did you put the groceries when you went into Mrs. Frazier's apartment?

FRANK *(Thinking):* Maybe I put them on the kitchen table, or on a chair. Let me see. . . . I was so shocked when I saw Mrs. Frazier lying on her bedroom floor—that's all I remember.

SALLY *(Slowly):* Hm-m. Tim didn't mention anything about finding a bag of groceries in her apartment.

FRANK: I left them there. *(Recollecting)* There was a bottle of milk, some butter, bread, and—oh, yes, I stopped at the bakery for some of those apple tarts Mrs. Frazier liked.

SALLY: Apple tarts?

FRANK *(Nodding):* Yes. Mrs. Frazier was expecting Mr. Bly for tea a little later on.

SALLY *(Reciting):*
The Queen of Hearts
She made some tarts
All on a summer's day—

FRANK *(Confused):* Nothing makes any sense.

SALLY: I think it makes a lot of sense. If you had killed Mrs. Frazier, you would never have left the bag of groceries behind.

FRANK *(Slowly):* I think I know what you're driving at. The murderer didn't want to make it too obvious that I had been in the apartment, so he took the groceries.

SALLY: That's right. Tim didn't mention anything about finding the apple tarts or the other things. That would mean—

FRANK *(Interrupting):* That the murderer came back a second time, after I was there, and took the groceries away!

SALLY: That's the way it must have happened. You didn't wear the jacket until the *second* time you went to her place. While you were at the store, somebody took your jacket, killed Mrs. Frazier, put the pearls into your pocket to incriminate you, then returned the jacket to your room.

FRANK *(Bitterly):* I'd like to make the police believe that.

SALLY *(Excitedly):* They'll have to believe it. Besides, Patty saw someone wearing your jacket. That someone killed Mrs. Frazier.

FRANK *(Surprised):* Patty saw the murder?

SALLY: What she saw, really, was a reflection in a looking glass. *(Pointing over parapet)* Mrs. Stevens's apartment is directly across from Mrs. Frazier's. Patty saw everything in Mrs. Stevens's mirror. She couldn't see the murderer's face, but she saw him holding a gun.

FRANK: If Patty saw the murderer wearing my jacket, that proves it was a deliberate frame-up. *(He pauses.)* It had to be someone who saw me leave for the store and knew I was going back to Mrs. Frazier's apartment. He killed Mrs. Frazier and planted the pearls in my jacket. *(Suddenly realizing he is still holding pearls, he puts them into his pocket.)*

SALLY: And then he put the jacket back in your room. . . . (FRANK *nods.*) The murderer has to be someone in this building.

FRANK: It's hard to believe, but I guess you're right. *(Snaps fingers)* Wait a minute! When I went back to my room to get my jacket, your mother was in the living room with Mr. Bly!

SALLY *(Thinking out loud):* He could have taken your jacket, committed the murder, put the pearls in the pocket, and then put the jacket back in your room before you got back with the groceries. She'd be going back and forth to the kitchen while she was making tea, and wouldn't even notice what he was doing.

FRANK: It could have been someone else, too.

SALLY: That's true, but there's something about Mr. Bly that frightens me.

FRANK: I think I'll have a talk with him.

SALLY: He just went out to get the paper.

FRANK: Good! That will give me a chance to search his apartment before he gets back.

SALLY *(Alarmed):* No, Frank. That's too dangerous. I don't trust him.

FRANK: I'll have to take the chance. His window is three

floors down—below this fire escape. *(He climbs onto fire escape.)*

SALLY *(Worriedly)*: Be careful, Frank!

FRANK *(As he starts down)*: It's dark. Maybe no one will see me. *(Softly)* I'm glad you still believe in me, Sally.

SALLY *(Tenderly)*: We still have our kingdom on the rooftop. *(She takes his hand briefly, then FRANK exits, down fire escape. Shortly, PATTY enters, eating an apple tart.)*

PATTY: Mom's waiting for you, Sally. *(SALLY turns quickly.)*

SALLY *(Confused)*: Oh, Patty, you frightened me. I'll go down in a minute.

PATTY: Why are you standing near the fire escape?

SALLY: No reason.

PATTY *(Joining her)*: I hear something down there. *(She looks over parapet.)*

SALLY *(Quickly)*: There's no one there, Patty.

PATTY: I can see someone on the fire escape.

SALLY *(Moving PATTY aside; nervously)*: I'm sure it's only a cat.

PATTY *(Turning to face SALLY)*: That was Frank, and you helped him escape!

SALLY: Please, Patty, don't tell anyone. He didn't kill Mrs. Frazier. Somebody's trying to frame him.

PATTY: Then why doesn't he tell Tim?

SALLY: Frank wants to work things out for himself first. *(Notices tart in PATTY's hand.)* What are you eating?

PATTY: This? It's an apple tart. Mom had them for dessert.

SALLY *(Excitedly)*: Where did she get them?

PATTY: At the store, I guess.

SALLY: Quick! Get Mom! Find out where she got those tarts. It's very important.

PATTY *(Bewildered)*: I don't get it, but I'll ask her.

SALLY *(Urgently)*: And Patty, don't tell *anyone* that Frank was here.

PATTY: All right, Sally, if that's what you want. *(SALLY hugs her. PATTY exits. As SALLY paces nervously, MR. BLY enters.)*

BLY: I was hoping to find you alone.

SALLY *(Nervously):* Mr. Bly! I thought you went for the newspaper. *(She moves downstage; he follows her.)*

BLY: No, that was just an excuse to leave while the others were still here. I wanted to speak to you alone.

SALLY *(Nervously):* What do you want? *(Backs away)*

BLY: Your mother told me you're interested in Frank.

SALLY: I'd rather not discuss that.

BLY: Your young man is in a great deal of trouble.

SALLY *(Defiantly):* Frank isn't a murderer.

BLY: Will the police believe that?

SALLY: They must believe it.

BLY *(Smiling):* And I want them to believe it, too. You see, I *know* Frank didn't kill Mrs. Frazier.

SALLY: You do? Mr. Bly, do you know who the murderer is?

BLY: I think so.

SALLY: You should go to the police.

BLY: Would they believe the suspicions of an eccentric old man? I have no proof.

SALLY *(Interrupting anxiously):* What is it, Mr. Bly? Please tell me!

BLY: When I visited your mother last night, I noticed something.

MRS. MURPHY *(Shouting from offstage):* Stop, murderer! There he is—on the fire escape!

SALLY: It's Frank! Mrs. Murphy's seen him. *(She rushes to parapet.)*

MRS. MURPHY *(Offstage):* Call the police!

SALLY: Oh, no! (SALLY *turns, grabs* BLY's *arm.*) What did you see last night? Quick—tell me!

BLY: I won't tell you. If the murderer knows I saw him, there's no saying what he'll do. *(Suddenly)* Is that police officer still with your mother?

SALLY: Yes.

BLY *(Interrupting):* I must see him.

SALLY: No, please! He'll arrest Frank. (BLY *exits right.* FRANK *leaps onto roof from fire escape.*)

FRANK *(Breathlessly):* The Murphys saw me trying to get
  into Bly's apartment.
SALLY: What are we going to do?
FRANK: I'm going to find Tim.
SALLY: Please wait. Bly was here. He said he might be able
  to help you.
FRANK: Bly? But I think he's the one who left the pearls in
  my pocket.
SALLY *(Shaking head):* He thinks you're innocent.
FRANK *(Angrily):* I'm tired of what people think about me.
  I'm going to take my chances with the law. *(He starts off
  right, and* SALLY *follows.)* No, Sally, stay here. I'd rather
  talk to Tim alone.
SALLY *(Resigned):* All right, Frank. I'll wait here for you.
  *(He exits right. Loud voices are heard from offstage. Roof door
  opens and* FRANK *re-enters, dejectedly.)* Frank, what's the
  matter?
FRANK *(Bitterly):* Bly is dead. His body's lying at the foot of
  the stairs leading to the roof.
SALLY: No! What happened?
FRANK: It looks as though he was thrown down the stairs.
  That'll clinch the case against me.
SALLY *(Quickly):* Whoever killed Mrs. Frazier had to silence
  Bly. The murderer realized that Bly saw something last
  night. Maybe the killer heard Bly talking to me.
FRANK: Tim won't buy that story.
SALLY *(Frightened):* What are we going to do?
FRANK *(Shrugging):* I can't run away—and I can't give my-
  self up. Tim will come for me. He'll be here in a few
  minutes. Murphy is screaming his head off in the courtyard.
SALLY: Oh, Frank—(FRANK *suddenly puts his hand across her
  mouth for a moment, to silence her. With his free hand, he points
  to roof door.)*
FRANK: Shh! I hear someone coming. (FRANK *goes right,
  hides behind door.* SALLY *watches doorway nervously.* LEFTY
  enters and walks toward her.)

SALLY *(Sighing with relief):* Lefty! You frightened me to death! For a moment, I thought you were . . .

LEFTY *(Quickly):* What did you think?

SALLY *(Taking his arm):* You've always been a good friend of Frank's. You must help him now.

LEFTY *(Coldly):* How can I help a murderer? (SALLY *drops his arm and steps back.*) Tell me. Where's Frank hiding?

SALLY: I haven't seen him.

LEFTY: You were never very good at lying.

SALLY: If you're going to talk like that about Frank, you'd better go. *(Thoughtfully)* Why did you come here, anyway?

LEFTY: You're a smart girl. You've probably figured that one out.

SALLY: I don't know what you're talking about.

LEFTY: Maybe you don't know anything about the apple tart, either.

SALLY *(Frightened):* The apple tart?

LEFTY: Yes, the apple tart that you saw Patty eating a little while ago. You told her to find out where your mother got it.

SALLY: How do you know that?

LEFTY: I'm pretty smart. I figured that you must have seen your boyfriend, and he told you he bought those tarts for Mrs. Frazier last night. You probably knew the murderer took them from Mrs. Frazier's place and put them in your mother's apartment.

SALLY *(Horrified):* You! It was you! You killed Mrs. Frazier! *(He grabs her arm with his left hand.)* And you killed Mr. Bly, too!

LEFTY: Bly was a meddlesome old fool. What did he tell you?

SALLY *(Terrified):* He didn't have time to tell me anything, but I think he saw you go into Frank's bedroom and leave the checkered jacket there after you killed Mrs. Frazier. He probably saw you put the pearls into Frank's pocket. *(Points right)* You were listening outside the door. You heard Bly say that he was going to the police, so when he left me, you killed him.

LEFTY *(Sarcastically):* That's a nice story. But who'll believe you?

SALLY: And you tried to frighten Patty, too. You watched her all day because you were nervous.

LEFTY: Patty is my key witness. She saw Frank commit the murder, remember?

SALLY: Yes, Patty will remember. She'll also remember we saw Mrs. Frazier's room in the mirror. You recognized the dresser and the hat boxes on the bed. But how could you know about the hat boxes unless you were there last night?

LEFTY *(Menacingly):* There are ways of taking care of troublesome people. (LEFTY *pulls* SALLY *by the arm with his left hand.*)

SALLY *(Excitedly):* Patty saw someone wearing Frank's coat. She saw the gun in his hand. (SALLY *points at* LEFTY'S *left arm clutching her arm.*) That proves you're the killer!

LEFTY *(Scornfully):* Where's your proof?

SALLY: Patty thought she saw someone holding a gun in his right hand shoot Mrs. Frazier. She really saw his reflection in the big mirror in Mrs. Stevens's bedroom. It appeared that the murderer used his right hand, but he was actually lefthanded!

LEFTY: I don't get it.

SALLY: I was a fool not to think of it before. If you stand in front of a mirror holding something in your right hand, it will look as if it's in your left hand. Frank is righthanded. If he killed Mrs. Frazier, Patty would have seen his reflection holding the gun in his left hand!

LEFTY *(Scornfully):* A pretty little theory, but you won't live to tell anyone about it.

SALLY: No matter what you do to me, someone will be able to put these facts together, too. Someone will remember that a reflection in a looking glass is always opposite to the real thing. You're the only lefthanded person involved in this case. You had access to Frank's bedroom. You could have taken his jacket, killed Mrs. Frazier, and returned the jacket to his room with the pearls in his pocket. That's what Mr. Bly saw while he was visiting Mom.

LEFTY *(Angrily):* You're pretty smart! O.K. I killed her. I killed them both. That old dame had plenty of money, and I was sick of living in a grubby room. I knew Mrs. Frazier liked Frank, and I had a chance to get even with him, too. He's always been the fair-haired boy around this house.

SALLY: You won't get away with it. Why, Patty's probably telling Tim what she saw right now! Tim will figure it out.

LEFTY *(Gesturing):* It's only a short jump across the court onto the next roof. I have most of the dough, although I hid some in my room. The police will think that Frank put it there. (LEFTY *pulls* SALLY *toward parapet. She screams. They struggle.* FRANK *comes from behind door.*)

FRANK *(Grabbing* LEFTY): Lefty! Let her go! (LEFTY *releases* SALLY *and whirls on* FRANK. FRANK *grapples with* LEFTY, *but* LEFTY *gives* FRANK *violent shove.* FRANK *loses his footing.* LEFTY *climbs onto fire escape, descends behind parapet.* TIM *enters.*)

TIM: Stop! *(He rushes to parapet.* FRANK *gets to his feet and they join* TIM *at parapet.)*

FRANK: He's getting away!

SALLY: Oh, Tim, it was Lefty! He killed Mrs. Frazier *and* Mr. Bly. Don't let him escape.

TIM: He won't get far. My men are surrounding the place. *(Loud crash is heard from offstage.)*

FRANK: Look! Mrs. Murphy hit Lefty over the head with a flowerpot!

TIM *(Pointing):* And there's one of my men climbing the

fire escape to get Lefty. *(He turns.)* I'd better get down there—fast! *(Grimly)* I just found Bly's body. *(To* FRANK) You'd better come down to headquarters. We'll need a statement.

SALLY *(Protesting):* But he's innocent!

TIM: I know. I looked through Lefty's room a little while ago and found some money in his suitcase. I also stood outside that door *(Pointing)* and heard enough to know that he's the killer.

SALLY: Oh Frank! Thank goodness you're safe now!

TIM: Yes, you don't need to hide any longer. I'll meet you down at Mom's place (TIM *exits right.*)

FRANK *(Taking* SALLY's *hand):* You've been wonderful, Sally, about everything. You had faith in me, and, well, what else can a man ask for?

SALLY *(Smiling):* I couldn't let anyone take our wonderland away! *(They embrace, as curtain falls.)*

THE END

Production Notes

THE LOOKING GLASS MURDER

Characters: 4 male; 6 female.

Playing time: 35 minutes.

Costumes: Everyday modern dress. Tess wears a wristwatch. Tim wears a police officer's uniform. Frank wears a checkered sport coat, and Mr. Bly is dressed in dark, shabby clothes.

Properties: A bag of green peas, pan, notebook, pencil, string of pearls and apple tart.

Setting: The rooftop of an apartment house. Upstage is a brick parapet about three feet high which runs the entire length of the stage. The parapet should be about six feet from the rear of the stage so that an effect of depth is created. In the center of the main parapet is a fire escape by which characters may exit. A door is at right and it should remain open so the characters can hide easily behind it as indicated in text. There are two chairs down center and potted plants down right. If desired, a backdrop of a city skyline may be used, and clotheslines, TV antennas, etc., may complete the setting.

Lighting: No special effects.

Sound: Voices; loud crash, as indicated in text.

Dead of Night

Characters

TIM, *a young antique shop owner*
SALLY, *his wife*
MR. HOLMES, *their friend*
CLAY STYLES, *about 23*
POLLY, *his fiancée*
MISS WILSON, *middle-aged nurse*
VOICE, *on tape*

TIME: *Late at night.*

SETTING: *A large room in Hector Styles's house, filled with old chairs, cabinets, tables, other furnishings, and bric-a-brac, all tagged for an auction. There is a raised platform down left, on which a table is standing. To the right of the platform is a cassette player. A chair and sofa are at center. There are entrances up center, right and left. Fireplace in left wall has artificial fire.*

AT RISE: SALLY *is examining furniture with interest.* TIM *is standing at table on auctioneer's platform.*

TIM (*Pounding gavel on table*): And now, ladies and gentlemen, to open this auction from the Hector Styles mansion, we have the treat of the day—(*Holds up object*) this rare collector's item, a genuine handwrought, eighteenth-century thingamabob! What am I offered? (*Points gavel at* SALLY) Do I hear $7.83? (*Pounds table*) Sold to the young lady with the cute, turned-up nose, who happens to be my wife! (SALLY *laughs.* TIM *puts gavel on table, steps off platform and hurries over to* SALLY, *bumping into bric-a-brac and nearly upsetting it.*)

SALLY: Tim, please be careful! If these things get broken, Mr. Holmes will have our hides.

TIM: I can't help it, Sally. I'm so excited about the auction tomorrow—I want to bid on everything here!

SALLY: This will be our first big auction, and if we can get some of these things, we'll have the best antique shop in town.

TIM: In fact, we'll have the *only* antique shop in Ackerman Falls.

SALLY: Mr. Holmes was wonderful to let us stay here tonight to look over the things beforehand.

TIM: A lot of this stuff is pretty expensive.

SALLY: I know, but we have enough money to bid on some of the small items.

TIM *(Nodding):* Old Hector Styles must have been worth a fortune.

SALLY: I always felt sorry for him, living in this lonely old house with only his nurse.

TIM: Right. *(Looks around)* The old man had everything— and yet he had nothing.

SALLY: And as for his nephew, Clay Styles! He should be ashamed of himself for neglecting his uncle. He didn't visit until he heard he was Mr. Styles's heir.

TIM: Oh, Clay's not so bad. You know, we were pretty good friends as kids. I understand he went to Europe after college, and I guess he was working on something over there.

SALLY: That may be, but . . . *(Slowly)* Tim, I wonder what really happened to Hector Styles?

TIM *(Surprised):* What do you mean?

SALLY: Everyone knew that he was ill, but *(Hesitating)* he did die rather suddenly.

TIM: I don't know what you're getting at.

SALLY: Even Dr. Waring was surprised Mr. Styles died so unexpectedly. Heart disease, they said, but Dr. Waring thought Mr. Styles had a strong heart for a man his age.

TIM: So what? Doctors have been wrong before. Have you been listening to the town gossips?

SALLY *(Insistently):* Well, there are people who feel that Hector met with foul play!

TIM: That's nonsense! Just because you're going to spend the night in a gloomy mansion doesn't mean that you have to be so melodramatic!

SALLY *(Stubbornly):* I'm not being melodramatic, but *(Glances around uneasily)* this house gives me the creeps. (MR. HOLMES *enters left.*)

HOLMES: Hello, there! Is there anything you like?

SALLY: Oh, hello, Mr. Holmes! We're so glad you let us come tonight. There are some excellent pieces here.

HOLMES: Fine! Fine! After all, you've always been my favorite young people.

TIM *(With sweeping gesture):* Is this *everything* to be auctioned?

HOLMES: Oh, no! I have the complete inventory in the library. There's some silverware, some very old damask, and a lot of other items.

TIM: I'd like to see the list. There may be other things we could bid on.

HOLMES: I'll be glad to show it to you.

SALLY *(Slowly, to* HOLMES): Can you tell us anything about Hector Styles?

HOLMES *(Shrugging):* There's very little to tell. He was a very rich man, and Clay Styles is his sole heir. Of course, there's Miss Wilson, his nurse, but except for a small bequest, everything goes to Clay. That's why Clay is here now. When the things are sold tomorrow, the estate can be settled.

SALLY: I didn't mean that. Do you know anything *personal* about Mr. Styles? What was he like?

HOLMES: Hector lived a simple life. I visited him a few times when he drew up his will. He was confined to a wheelchair, and he hadn't left the grounds for the past ten years. Yes, Hector was a lonely old man.

SALLY: Do you think anything odd could have happened to him?

HOLMES *(Puzzled):* What do you mean?

TIM: Oh, Sally, don't start that again!

SALLY *(Insistently):* People in town think he was—murdered!

HOLMES *(Strongly):* What an insane idea! Why, Miss Wilson was the only one here when he died. And, anyway, who would possibly want to murder Hector Styles?

SALLY: But the rumors—

HOLMES: Oh, I'm used to small–town gossip. I've heard it all, and I'm convinced that Hector Styles died a natural death.

TIM *(To* SALLY*):* I told you that talk was idle gossip. *(To* HOLMES*)* May I see that auction list now?

SALLY *(Resigned):* Oh, I'm sorry I mentioned it. Please go on, Tim. I'm going to stay here and look over some more of these pieces. (HOLMES *and* TIM *exit.* SALLY *walks around room, examining various pieces of furniture. She picks up cassette recorder, looks at it closely.*) A cassette player! Why, it looks new. This is no antique. I wonder what's on this tape. *(Presses button; classical music is heard. After a moment, music stops, and* VOICE *is heard on tape.)*

VOICE *(From cassette recorder; urgently):* This is Hector Styles. Please listen to me. I can't leave this house, and I am afraid to use the telephone, because he may overhear my conversation. *(Pauses.* SALLY *looks puzzled.)* This tape is my only chance to tell someone what is happening here. No one suspects that my nephew, Clay Styles, is in this country, in this house! I don't know why he has come, but I think he wants to kill me. I'm afraid my food may be poisoned. If anything happens to me, turn this tape over to the police. Arrest Clay Styles for my murder! *(Music resumes on tape.)*

SALLY *(Shocked; to herself):* I can't believe it! *(She pushes another button, and tape starts to rewind.)* I have to hear this again. (CLAY STYLES *enters and crosses to* SALLY. *She does not hear him.)*

CLAY: Hello, Sally! *(She jumps back, in surprise.)*

SALLY *(Frightened):* Oh, Clay! Clay Styles! I didn't recognize you at first. How—how long have you been here?

CLAY: A few seconds. I was in the garden. *(Suspicious)* What's the matter?

SALLY *(Quickly):* Nothing! Nothing at all! You startled me, that's all. *(She looks quickly at recorder.)*

CLAY: That's the cassette recorder I sent Uncle Hector a few months ago. I guess he never had much chance to use it.

SALLY *(Thoughtfully):* No—I guess he was too sick.

CLAY *(Puzzled):* I wonder what it's doing in here? I doubt an antique dealer would want it. (CLAY *moves closer to recorder.* SALLY *tries to block* CLAY.) What were you playing?

SALLY: I—I don't know. I don't care for serious music.

CLAY: Sally, you're trembling. Is something wrong?

SALLY: No!

CLAY *(Irritated):* Look, Sally. I don't know what's come over you or the folks in this town. You look at me as though you're afraid of me.

SALLY *(Quickly):* Afraid? Oh, no.

CLAY: Oh, come off it. You're like the others. Suspicious because I didn't stay here with Uncle Hector. Well, *he* sent me away, wanted me to study in Europe. I didn't desert him. You must believe that.

SALLY: But you never came back. Not until now.

CLAY *(Nodding):* That's right, not for ten years.

SALLY: You weren't here when he was—when he died?

CLAY: Of course not! Why do you ask?

SALLY *(Quickly):* Oh, nothing!

CLAY *(Sharply):* You know very well that Polly and I got to Ackerman Falls only two days ago. What made you think I was here when Uncle Hector died? What are you trying to suggest?

SALLY: Please, Clay—

CLAY: Tell me, Sally—do you think I had anything to do with my uncle's death?

SALLY: No! Of course not!

CLAY *(Grabbing* SALLY's *arm):* Listen to me. I don't know how those stories started or who started them, but something is wrong in this town, and I'm going to find the person who's against me. (SALLY *pulls away.* TIM *enters left, doesn't notice* CLAY.)

TIM: Sally, there's some old tableware I'd like you to see, and—*(Sees* CLAY*)* Hello, Clay. It's been ages since I last saw you.

CLAY *(Angrily):* No, but you've apparently been hearing plenty about me from Sally. I've had enough. *(Exits quickly)*

TIM: What's the matter with him?

SALLY *(Quickly):* He—Clay—killed Hector Styles!

TIM: Not that again! Sally, you have to stop this.

SALLY: I have proof! *(Points to recorder)* I found a tape recording by Hector Styles, accusing Clay of murdering him.

TIM *(Alarmed):* Does anyone else know about the tape?

SALLY: No, I don't think so. Clay came in when I was playing it, but I don't think he heard it. (TIM *goes to recorder.)* What are we going to do?

TIM: We'd better put the cassette in a safe place, for starters. If Clay knew about it, he'd do anything to get hold of it. (TIM *takes cassette from recorder and puts it on table. Hand reaches in through doorway and turns off light switch. Stage is darkened.* SALLY *screams. Running footsteps are heard. In the darkness,* TIM *crosses to switch and turns lights*

on. SALLY *is still by recorder, rubbing her head as if dazed.*
MISS WILSON *is standing in center entrance.)*
MISS WILSON *(Entering):* What happened?
TIM *(Quickly):* Miss Wilson, did you see anyone in the hall?
MISS WILSON: No, I was going to the kitchen, when I heard
some noise in here. *(To* SALLY) Are you hurt, Sally?
SALLY *(Weakly):* Someone bumped into me, but I'm all
right. *(Looks at recorder)* The cassette! Tim, it's gone! The
cassette's been stolen!
TIM: Whoever took it must have gone out through the
garden. I'll take a look. *(Exits right)*
MISS WILSON: How terrible! Is there anything I can do?
SALLY: You might be able to help, Miss Wilson. *(Abruptly)*
Were you here when Mr. Styles died?
MISS WILSON *(Sadly):* Yes, I lost a good friend. I was his
nurse for a long time.
SALLY *(Hesitantly):* Was there anything unusual about his
death?
MISS WILSON: No, he died in his sleep. Dr. Waring said it
was a massive coronary.
SALLY *(Slowly):* But there are people in town who think he
was murdered.
MISS WILSON: Yes, I've heard those stories, too. No one
killed Hector Styles. I—I was alone with him when he
died.
SALLY *(Insistently):* Are you certain there was no one else in
the house?
MISS WILSON *(Sharply):* Of course I am. *(Slowly)* But it is a
very large place.
SALLY *(Quickly):* Then someone might have been here
without your knowledge?
MISS WILSON: Yes, I suppose that's possible.
SALLY: Did you leave the house shortly after Mr. Styles's
death?
MISS WILSON: Yes. Mr. Holmes, the attorney, stayed here

with me for three days, making an inventory of what would be auctioned, then we left. He thought it would be better if I stayed in town until the estate was settled. Yesterday, he asked me to attend the auction. He told me that before the auction, I could take something as a memento.

SALLY: Then the house has been empty since Hector Styles's death?

MISS WILSON: Yes. I came back here yesterday for the first time in six months.

SALLY: Just when did Mr. Styles die?

MISS WILSON: It was a Sunday morning, March twenty-second. I left the house with Mr. Holmes on Wednesday, the twenty-fifth. I remember everything that happened that sad day.

SALLY *(Nodding):* That was six months ago. I wish we could be sure no one had entered the house since he died.

MISS WILSON: I don't think anything is missing. Mr. Holmes has the complete list of valuables, and he would have mentioned any theft. *(Abruptly)* Sally, I wish you'd tell me what happened here. (TIM *enters right.*)

TIM: Well, whoever turned off the lights and stole the cassette has escaped without a trace. I couldn't even find any footprints.

MISS WILSON: Cassette? *(She notices recorder.)* Clay sent Mr. Styles the tape recorder as a gift, but he never lived to enjoy it. It arrived the morning after his death.

SALLY *(Startled):* What? (TIM *cautions* SALLY *to silence, as* MISS WILSON *continues.*)

MISS WILSON: But what is the tape recorder doing here? I left it in the library. *(Shrugs)* We'll probably never know. I hope you'll excuse me. It's been a long day, and I'm tired. It must be well after midnight. *(Looks fondly around room)* There are so many memories here. So many sad memories. *(Exits center)*

SALLY: Did you hear what she said about the tape player?

That it arrived after Mr. Styles died? It can't be true.

TIM: I know. It's very strange.

SALLY *(Slowly):* If we believe her, the recording would have been made by a *dead man!*

TIM: Maybe she's wrong about the date the tape recorder arrived.

SALLY: Or she might be lying.

TIM: Why should she lie? She doesn't benefit by Hector's will. *(Quickly)* We have to find that cassette—if it hasn't been destroyed. And meantime, don't tell anyone about what you heard.

SALLY: Somebody else should know.

TIM *(Quickly):* Not yet. Whoever took the cassette wanted to destroy Hector Styles's evidence. If the person behind this business knew that you heard it, you'd be in real danger.

SALLY *(Helplessly):* But whoever took it must have guessed that I heard the message!

TIM: That's why I'm not going to leave you alone.

SALLY *(Calmly):* Don't worry, Tim. I'll be all right.

TIM: Murdered men who make recordings—thieves who steal from under our very noses—I don't like it! (POLLY *enters center.*)

POLLY: Oh, hi. I thought Clay was here.

SALLY: Hi, Polly. He was here a little while ago, but he left.

TIM: Isn't he in his room?

POLLY: No, I knocked on his door, but he didn't answer. *(Slowly)* It's so strange.

SALLY: What's strange?

POLLY: Clay's room is next to mine, and I'm sure I heard his closet door close. It makes a very loud noise. Clay and I have mentioned it before. But when I knocked, there was no answer.

SALLY: I'm sure he's somewhere in the house—or maybe the garden.

POLLY: I don't think so. *(Angrily)* I wish I'd never come to this dreadful town. Everyone thinks that Clay killed his uncle. I saw the way the people in town looked at him. It's so unfair. Clay loved his uncle. He's been so upset. We were supposed to be married in a few months, but Clay will never marry me, not when people are saying that he's a murderer.

TIM: I know it's been rough for you, Polly. Maybe we'll— *(Breaks off)* Did you say you heard someone in Clay's room—but you didn't get an answer when you knocked? *(She nods.)* That gives me an idea. *(To* SALLY) Sally, stay here with Polly. I'll be right back. *(Exits center)*

POLLY: Where is he going?

SALLY: I'm not sure, but I have a pretty good hunch. *(Crosses to sofa and sits)* You love Clay, don't you?

POLLY: Oh, yes! He wanted me to go back home to London, but I'm going to stay right here. I know that he didn't kill his uncle, and I want to see it cleared up.

SALLY *(Quickly):* Was Clay in London when his uncle died?

POLLY: Why, yes! Miss Wilson called Clay's hotel and left a message. It was a Sunday afternoon.

SALLY: Was he in London the week before his uncle died?

POLLY: Yes. *(Pauses)* He was away for a few days, though. He went to the University to register for the summer session.

SALLY: Did you hear from him during that time?

POLLY: No, but he was gone for only two or three days.

SALLY: Then it's possible that he might have gone somewhere else—not to the University at all.

POLLY *(Upset):* It's possible, but why do you ask? Do you think he might have been in Ackerman Falls?

SALLY: I didn't say that.

POLLY *(Sharply):* I thought you and Tim were our friends. Instead, you're trying to build a case against Clay! You're like everyone else—prying—asking questions— suspicious. No matter what, Clay and I will see this thing through. *(Two gunshots, followed by screams, are heard off-stage.* SALLY *jumps up.* MISS WILSON *enters with* TIM, *who assists her to the sofa.* TIM *holds cassette, which he places on table nearby.)*

SALLY: What happened?

MISS WILSON *(Almost hysterical):* Someone tried to kill me!

TIM *(Grimly):* That's true. I found Miss Wilson at the foot of the stairs.

MISS WILSON *(Excitedly):* I came out of the kitchen and started to go upstairs. I thought I heard something on the first landing. Suddenly, I saw a hand and a gun come out of the darkness. Then, I don't know what happened. I heard some shots.

POLLY: Are you hurt?

MISS WILSON: No, the bullets hit the wall above my head.

SALLY: How horrible!

TIM: Did you recognize the person?

MISS WILSON: No, it was too dark.

SALLY: I'm going to call the police.

TIM: You can't. The phone was disconnected after Mr. Styles's death.

POLLY *(Jumping up, agitated):* What are we going to do? Someone is trying to kill us.

SALLY *(Slowly):* There's a murderer in this house. *(Pause)* I wonder why Mr. Holmes didn't hear the shots.

TIM: I left him in the library, and I understand it's soundproof.

MISS WILSON: Yes, Mr. Styles had it built so he could listen to his records without being disturbed. *(Weeps)*

POLLY: I'll take you to your room, Miss Wilson.

MISS WILSON: Yes, I'd like to rest. (POLLY *helps* MISS WILSON *to her feet. They exit center.)*

SALLY: Where's Clay? Did you find anything in his room? (TIM *takes cassette from table and hands it to* SALLY.) I'll bet this is the cassette I heard. Where did you find it?

TIM: It was in the closet in Clay's room.

SALLY: Then it was Clay who stole the tape!

TIM: I'm afraid so. He didn't know you'd heard it, and he must have stolen it to prevent you from playing it. *(Shaking his head)* I liked Clay. *(Soberly)* I didn't want to believe that he was a murderer.

SALLY: He might be outside—watching us! Oh, Tim, I'm afraid!

TIM: Don't worry. I won't let anything happen to you. *(Footsteps are heard from off right.)* I hear someone coming. Sh-h-h! *(They tiptoe to right entrance and stand on either side of it. CLAY rushes in. His suit is soiled. He holds his hand against his head, weaves slightly, as if faint. TIM crosses to him, helps him to sofa.)* Clay, what happened to you? Where have you been?

CLAY *(Sullenly):* Taking a walk. Is there any law against that?

TIM: No, but you could have entered through the front door, shot at Miss Wilson, and escaped into the garden again.

CLAY *(Shouting):* Shot Miss Wilson! *(Angrily)* What are you talking about? *(He rubs his head.)*

SALLY *(To TIM):* Clay's hurt. He's bleeding. *(TIM examines the wound on CLAY's head.)*

TIM: How did you get that wound?

CLAY: I heard someone running around the side of the house. I called out—and wham, that's all I remember.

SALLY *(Looking at wound):* We'd better take care of that.

CLAY *(Pulling away from her):* I don't need your help.

SALLY *(To TIM):* Clay couldn't have done this to himself.

TIM: Oh, no? Murderers have been known to wound themselves to throw off suspicion.

CLAY *(Sarcastically):* Thanks! *(TIM walks to table and picks up cassette. He turns to CLAY.)*

TIM: What do you know about this cassette?

CLAY *(Shrugging):* I guess it came with the tape recorder I sent Uncle Hector. I sent him several classical music cassettes.

TIM: Did you take this cassette off the recorder earlier tonight?

CLAY: Of course not! What would I want with it?

TIM (*To* SALLY): He just may be telling the truth, Sally—but I'm not taking any chances. (TIM *puts cassette on table, pulls* CLAY *to his feet, holding* CLAY'*s arm firmly.*) C'mon, Clay. I'm going to have another look in your room.

CLAY: *Another* look? Have you searched my room?

TIM: Yes, I found that cassette in your closet.

CLAY: I don't know anything about that. I put my things in the closet today, and there was no cassette there then.

TIM: Don't play dumb. The cassette was stolen from this room—a little while ago!

CLAY *(Insistently):* But I was in the garden.

TIM: Very convenient! (HOLMES *enters briskly left, keeping his right hand in his pocket. He crosses room, sees cassette on table, stops.*)

HOLMES: What's going on here?

TIM: I'll explain everything later, Mr. Holmes. Right now, Clay and I are going upstairs. Please keep an eye on Sally. (TIM *and* CLAY *exit center.*)

HOLMES: Is something wrong?

SALLY *(Sighing):* I'm afraid so. We think Clay may have killed his uncle.

HOLMES *(Shocked):* What? I don't believe it!

SALLY: I don't want to believe it, either, but—*(Suddenly)* say, you don't know that someone tried to kill Miss Wilson, do you?

HOLMES: What? This is terrible! *(After a pause)* Do you really think Clay could be a murderer?

SALLY *(Shaking head):* The whole thing has me puzzled. I don't see why Clay would want to kill Miss Wilson. She doesn't benefit from Hector Styles's will, does she?

HOLMES *(Shaking head):* No. Clay is the sole beneficiary.

SALLY: Who would be the beneficiary if anything happened to Clay? Isn't it true that a man convicted of murder cannot inherit property from his victim?

HOLMES *(Slowly):* Yes, I believe that's true.

SALLY: Then, someone might want us to *think* that Clay killed his uncle, someone who would then inherit the Styles fortune. *(Snaps fingers)* Of course! That's it! Someone is trying to frame Clay for murder!

HOLMES *(Quickly):* Don't let your imagination go too far!

SALLY *(Continuing):* That same person who tried to kill Miss Wilson because she knew that the tape recorder didn't arrive at this house until the day *after* Hector Styles's death!

HOLMES: How do you know that?

SALLY: Miss Wilson told me. Her attacker didn't know it, though. He wanted to silence her before she ruined his plans.

HOLMES: That's hardly conclusive proof, Sally. After all, Styles might have owned a tape recorder of his own, and made the recording before Clay's gift arrived. Why, he might have—*(He stops as SALLY looks intently at him.)*

SALLY: How do you know about the tape recording?

HOLMES *(Nervously):* What tape recording?

SALLY: The one made by Hector Styles. *(Slowly)* I was the only person who heard it. I told Tim about it, but he hasn't heard it. No one else has.

HOLMES: I—I heard it playing while I was in the library.

SALLY: In a soundproof room? You said you didn't know anything about the attack on Miss Wilson. If you couldn't hear the shots, how could you possibly have heard the tape? (SALLY *backs away from* HOLMES, *moving toward table.)*

HOLMES *(Menacingly):* You're a very foolish young girl.

SALLY *(Quickly):* You shot at Miss Wilson, didn't you? You knew that if she remembered the exact date the tape recorder arrived, your trumped-up case against Clay would be useless. Miss Wilson told me that you stayed here for three days after Hector Styles's death.When the tape recorder arrived, you thought of a plan to cheat Clay out of his inheritance, and get the money for yourself.

HOLMES: That's nonsense! (*He takes a step toward* SALLY.)

SALLY: It's so clear now. Hector Styles died a natural death, after all. He was an old man. You knew that if Clay was convicted of his uncle's murder, he wouldn't receive the inheritance. And I'll bet that under Mr. Styles's will, you're the sole beneficiary after Clay.

HOLMES: You're making all of this up.

SALLY (*Breathlessly*): You made that recording! You knew old Mr. Styles so well that you could imitate his voice. You wanted everyone to hear him accuse Clay of murder!

HOLMES (*Scoffingly*): I suppose you can prove that!

SALLY: Yes, I can. If Clay had stolen the cassette accusing him of murder, he would have destroyed it immediately. You stole it and hid it in his closet, to throw suspicion on him. You couldn't let anything happen to the recording, because it was the only proof you had against Clay Styles!

HOLMES: I'm not the only one who thinks Clay is guilty.

SALLY: I'm sure you planted all those rumors. You had a great chance to circulate gossip.

HOLMES: I hope you're not planning to tell everyone this foolish theory of yours.

SALLY (*Defiantly*): I'm going to call Tim now. (HOLMES *takes gun out of his pocket.*)

HOLMES (*Menacingly*): I wouldn't advise that. You're pretty clever, Sally. I went to great pains to make the recording and set the tape recorder in this room. I won't let anything go wrong. (*He levels gun at* SALLY.)

SALLY: You wouldn't dare kill me. Tim is with Clay now. If anything happens to me, he'll know that Clay isn't a murderer.

HOLMES *(Nodding):* That's a possibility, but Clay might have a confederate in this affair. *(Smiles)* Yes, a confederate. I can tell them that a strange man tried to steal the cassette. I fought with him and—well—the gun went off. An unfortunate accident. You were killed. The cassette will be saved, of course. *(Grimly)* I'll see that it's played in court, against Clay Styles. *(Defiantly)* You were wrong, Sally. I am not the beneficiary, but I am the executor of Hector's estate, and if Clay is found guilty, there are many opportunities. . . .

SALLY: And you made that recording just to frame Clay.

HOLMES: Ingenious, don't you think? Any juror will render a "guilty" verdict when he hears the testimony of the murdered man. And Miss Wilson. She's such a nice woman—but I suppose I will have to dispose of her before the trial. An old lady—a fatal accident. Such a pity!

SALLY *(Horrified):* You wouldn't!

HOLMES: But I think we have talked much too long. *(He snaps safety catch off gun, puts on silencer.* SALLY *quickly grabs recording from table, backs away toward fireplace.)* What are you doing? Put that down!

SALLY: If—if you come near me, I'll burn this tape! *(She waves it threateningly.)* And that will be the end of your case against Clay.

HOLMES *(Hysterically):* Put that down!

SALLY: You should have kept this cassette, since it's the only shred of evidence you have against Clay. *(Gun shakes in* HOLMES's *hand.)* Are you frightened?

HOLMES *(Smoothly):* I think we can come to an arrangement that will satisfy us both.

SALLY *(Shaking head):* I'm afraid attempted murder isn't exactly my dish. *(Strongly)* I'll give you exactly thirty seconds to call Tim and Clay and tell them the whole story. Otherwise, this tape will go up in flames. You may kill me, but you'll never get the Styles fortune. (SALLY *holds cassette higher.* HOLMES *glares at her, aiming gun at her.*) HOLMES *(Coldly):* I've gone too far to be stopped. I won't let you stand in my way. (TIM *and* CLAY *rush in center, surprising* HOLMES, *who spins around to face them.* TIM *knocks the gun to floor.* CLAY *retrieves it and aims it at* HOLMES *as* TIM *pins* HOLMES'S *arms behind his back.* SALLY *places cassette on table and crosses to* TIM.)

SALLY *(Sobbing):* He tried to kill me. He—he wanted to kill Miss Wilson, too.

TIM *(Grimly):* You'd better take over, Clay. Keep this bird locked in the library until I get the police.

CLAY: It'll be a pleasure! *(He pushes* HOLMES *ahead of him. They exit left.)*

TIM: I guess we got here just in time. *(Puts arms around* SALLY) While I was searching Clay's room, he mentioned that Holmes would be in control of the estate if anything happened to him. *(Taps forehead)* Something suddenly clicked, and knowing you were alone with Holmes, well—we rushed right down.

SALLY: Darling, you're a genius! And what timing!

TIM: I'll have to drive to police headquarters. Want to come along?

SALLY: Nothing doing! I wouldn't miss this auction for the world.

TIM *(Smiling):* You're really something. You were almost killed, and you still think about the auction and our antique shop.

SALLY: I'm thinking about our future, too! (TIM *hugs* SALLY *as curtains close.*)

THE END

Production Notes

DEAD OF NIGHT

Characters: 3 male; 3 female.

Playing Time: 30 minutes.

Costumes: Everyday modern dress.

Properties: Gavel, tape of several seconds of classical music interrupted by message from Hector Styles (actually read by actor playing Mr. Holmes), gun.

Setting: A large room in an old mansion, with groups of chairs, tables, cabinets, other furniture, and bric-a-brac arranged around room. Tags hang from all furnishings. There is a raised auctioneer's platform down left, on which is a table with a gavel lying on it. To the right of the platform is a tape recorder with a tape on it, ready to play. A chair and sofa are at center. There is a fireplace with a fire burning in it in left wall. There are entrances up center, left and right. Light switch is near right entrance.

Lighting: Room lights go off and on, as indicated in text.

Sound: Gunshots.

The Sixth Juror

Characters

JEFF WILLARD, *prosecuting attorney*
JUDGE THOMPSON
WILLIAM SHANNON, *attorney for the defense*
MRS. MEREDITH
MRS. POTTS
CLAY TREVOR
SERGEANT TOLLIVER
ALICE BEDFORD
BRUCE COLLINS
EVERETT FRANKLIN
MISS AMANDA NETTLETON, *the sixth juror*
MRS. SHAW ⎱ *jurors*
MRS. PITNEY ⎰
CLERK OF THE COURT
OTHER JURORS
SPECTATORS

SETTING: *Courtroom in Sands Crossing, a small seaside community. Judge's bench is up center, on raised platform. There is small table for Clerk below and in front of platform. Witness stand is at right of Judge. Both face audience. Jury box is at right angle, facing audience. Defense and prosecution tables are left and right, facing audience. Spectators' gallery is down left.*

AT RISE: JUDGE THOMPSON *presides.* CLERK *is taking notes.* WILLIAM SHANNON *and* CLAY TREVOR, *his client, sit at table, left.* JEFF WILLARD *stands facing* JUDGE, *addressing the court.* AMANDA NETTLETON, MRS. SHAW, MRS. PITNEY *and* OTHER JURORS *sit up right, and* SPECTATORS, *including* MRS. MEREDITH, MRS. POTTS, ALICE BEDFORD, SERGEANT TOLLIVER, BRUCE COLLINS, *and* EVERETT FRANKLIN, *sit down left.* MISS NETTLETON, *an elderly woman, knits during proceedings.*

WILLARD: And it is the purpose of this preliminary hearing to establish beyond any reasonable doubt that on the afternoon of July 28th, Clay Trevor *(Points to* CLAY*)* did willfully murder his guardian, Alexander Brier. We will call witnesses who will establish that Clay Trevor had motive and opportunity to commit this crime and will demand that this case be bound over for the Grand Jury. We will—*(He pauses, and turns, annoyed, to look at* MISS NETTLETON. *He turns to* JUDGE THOMPSON.*)* If it please the court, the State would like to remind the sixth juror that this is a legal hearing and not a sewing circle! I find her knitting distracting and not befitting a conscientious juror.

THOMPSON: If juror number six will kindly put her knitting away. . . . *(*MISS NETTLETON *continues knitting.)* Miss Nettleton! *(She looks up quickly.)*

MISS NETTLETON: Yes, Amos? I mean, Your Honor?

THOMPSON: Mr. Willard would like you to stop knitting. He finds it distracting.

MISS NETTLETON: Fiddlesticks! Nothing is more soothing to the nerves than knitting. *(Waves her finger)* You should try knitting yourself, Jeff Willard. You're much too tense.

WILLARD *(Between clenched teeth):* The sixth juror is interrupting my opening address.

MISS NETTLETON *(Surprised):* The sixth juror? *(She looks around jury.)* Well, I guess I am the sixth juror, though I

don't know why you can't use my name. *(Sighs)* It seems
that everyone is identified by number these days. *(She
holds up her knitting.)* Give up my knitting? Never! You
see, knitting helps me think, and someone should certainly do that at this hearing! (THOMPSON *pounds gavel.*)
THOMPSON: There is nothing in the statute that prevents a
juror from knitting. *(To* MISS NETTLETON) Will you
please try to knit a little more quietly, Miss Nettleton?
MISS NETTLETON: Of course, Your Honor. The sweater is
almost finished, anyway. *(Proudly)* It's for my sister Hannah's boy.
WILLARD *(Impatiently):* Your Honor, may we get on without
further delay?
THOMPSON: Mr. Willard, I grant that this is highly irregular, but we must remember that Sands Crossing is—
ahem—a closely-knit community. Miss Nettleton, before
her retirement, taught most of us at our local high
school, and has taught some of our children, too. If
there are certain informalities in the proceedings, we
must show some patience.
WILLARD *(Regaining composure):* Yes, Your Honor. . . . The
State calls its first witness, Sergeant John Tolliver. (CLERK
rises and addresses SPECTATORS.)
CLERK: Sergeant John Tolliver will take the stand, please.
(SERGEANT TOLLIVER *approaches stand, pauses to take oath in
pantomime from* CLERK. TOLLIVER *takes seat in witness box.*
WILLARD *approaches.)*
WILLARD: Your name, please.
TOLLIVER: Sergeant John Tolliver, state trooper, stationed
at the Sands Crossing barracks.
WILLARD: You were on duty the afternoon of July 28th?
TOLLIVER: Yes, sir.
WILLARD: Will you tell the court what happened that
afternoon?
TOLLIVER: We received a call at 1:10 P.M. from Alexander
Brier's place out on Parrot Island.

WILLARD: Who made that call?

TOLLIVER: Ella Meredith, Mr. Brier's housekeeper. She said that Mr. Brier had been shot and asked us to come at once.

WILLARD: And you responded to the call?

TOLLIVER: Yes, sir. We took the police launch and reached the island in fifteen minutes.

WILLARD: For the record, will you tell us the exact location of Parrot Island?

MISS NETTLETON (*Interrupting*): Poppycock! Everyone in these parts knows where Parrot Island is, Jeff Willard. Why, you used to fish there when you played hooky from English class.

THOMPSON: Miss Nettleton, it is purely as a formality that the location of Parrot Island be clearly established in the records of this hearing.

WILLARD (*Angrily*): Let the record also show, Your Honor, that the sixth juror was asked to refrain from further remarks. (*Glares at* MISS NETTLETON, *then turns to* TOLLIVER) Continue, Sergeant.

TOLLIVER: Parrot Island is a small island owned by the late Mr. Brier. It lies in the bay, between Sands Crossing and the town of Lockwood.

WILLARD: Why did you take a police launch to the island? There's a main causeway to the island from Lockwood.

TOLLIVER: The causeway is located on the far end of the island, facing Lockwood. And that's more than fifteen miles away from Sands Crossing.

WILLARD: Please continue, Sergeant.

TOLLIVER: When we reached Parrot Island, we met Everett Franklin. He had just sailed across from the Lockwood marine base in his skiff.

WILLARD: Did Mr. Franklin say why he was on the island?

TOLLIVER: He had an appointment with Mr. Brier. We moored the boats at the landing bank and went immediately to the house. Of course, Mr. Franklin was alarmed to hear of Mr. Brier's accident, and accompanied us.

WILLARD: And what did you find at the Brier house?

TOLLIVER: The housekeeper, Mrs. Meredith, took us to the library, where we found the body of Alexander Brier. He had been shot—there was a bullet wound in the chest.

WILLARD: Let the record show that the autopsy found the bullet to have come from a .38 revolver. What happened then, Sergeant?

TOLLIVER: I phoned the coroner, and sent back to the barracks for more men. I stationed officers at the causeway approach to the island, and at the dock, so no one could leave.

WILLARD: Did you conduct a search of the island and the house?

TOLLIVER: Yes, sir. I searched the house myself.

WILLARD: Did you find anything unusual?

TOLLIVER (Nodding): I found a .38 revolver in one of the bedroom closets. It had been recently fired. (WILLARD crosses to CLERK's table, picks up gun marked with tag, and returns.)

WILLARD: Is this the gun you found? (TOLLIVER takes gun, examines it.)

TOLLIVER: Yes, sir. It's the .38 revolver I found.

WILLARD: You said you found the gun in one of the bedrooms. Whose bedroom was it?

TOLLIVER: Clay Trevor's bedroom. (SHANNON leaps to his feet.)

SHANNON: Objection! The allegation that the gun was found in my client's bedroom does not establish positive ownership.

CLAY (Rising): It's all right, Mr. Shannon. (To THOMPSON) I admit that I own a .38 revolver, but Mr. Brier always kept it in the library desk. I don't know how it got into my bedroom closet.

THOMPSON: Objection overruled. Proceed, Mr. Willard. (CLAY *and* SHANNON *sit.*)

WILLARD: I have no further questions, Your Honor.

SHANNON: No questions, Your Honor. (TOLLIVER *stands.* MISS NETTLETON *raises her hand, waves it timidly.*)

MISS NETTLETON: Amos—Your Honor—there's a little question I'd like to ask.

WILLARD *(Angrily):* Your Honor, we just can't have these interruptions!

THOMPSON *(To* WILLARD): It is not unusual for a juror to seek clarification from the bench at a preliminary hearing. *(To* MISS NETTLETON) Does your question have a direct bearing on Sergeant Tolliver's testimony?

MISS NETTLETON: Well, I certainly hope so. I'm not a criminologist, but there's something wrong here— definitely wrong. If I were a murderer and I wanted to dispose of a murder weapon in a hurry, and I had the entire Atlantic Ocean surrounding me, I'd never put the gun in my own bedroom closet.

THOMPSON: An interesting point.

MISS NETTLETON: But someone else might have hidden the gun there—to throw suspicion on Clay.

MRS. SHAW: Why, Amanda, I believe you're right.

MRS. PITNEY: Leave it to Amanda Nettleton to find the fly in the ointment!

MISS NETTLETON: You're very kind, Mrs. Pitney. *(Leaning forward)* Oh, by the way, how did my home remedy act on your mother's rheumatism?

MRS. PITNEY: Right as rain. She was up painting the barn yesterday. (THOMPSON *pounds with gavel.*)

THOMPSON *(Sternly):* Silence in the court! There will be no further outbursts from members of the jury.

WILLARD *(Angrily):* I call my second witness, Alice Bedford. (TOLLIVER *returns to gallery, and* ALICE BEDFORD *approaches bench, takes oath, sits in witness box.*) You are Alice

Bedford, personal secretary to the late Mr. Brier, are you not?

ALICE: That's right. I was employed by Mr. Brier for five years.

WILLARD: And you live in the house on Parrot Island?

ALICE: Yes.

WILLARD: Who else shared that house?

ALICE: Bruce Collins, Mr. Brier's nephew, Mrs. Meredith, our housekeeper, and Mrs. Potts, the cook and cleaning woman. And there's also—*(Her voice trails off.)*

THOMPSON: Will the witness raise her voice for the benefit of the court?

ALICE: I—I'm sorry.

WILLARD: Who else lives in the house?

ALICE: Clay Trevor.

WILLARD: Was he related to Mr. Brier?

ALICE: No. Clay's parents died when he was very young. His father was Mr. Brier's best friend. After his parents' death, Clay moved to Parrot Island, and Mr. Brier has been like a father to him since then.

WILLARD: So Clay Trevor was likely to inherit Brier's fortune? He had a motive?

ALICE *(Horrified):* No! No! How can you accuse Clay of such a terrible thing? *(To* CLAY; *emotionally)* Oh, Clay, I know you didn't do this—

THOMPSON *(Gently):* Miss Bedford, please—just answer the questions.

WILLARD: Now, Miss Bedford, did you handle Mr. Brier's legal affairs?

ALICE *(Sadly):* I am the executrix for the estate.

WILLARD: So the terms of the will are well known to you.

ALICE: Yes.

WILLARD: Shortly before he died, did Mr. Brier tell you that he wished to change his will?

ALICE *(Sarcastically):* I don't know why you're asking me

these questions. It's quite evident that Mrs. Meredith has given you a full account of my conversation with Mr. Brier. *(She points to* MRS. MEREDITH, *who sits in gallery.)* She'll be able to tell you everything that happened in the house.

MRS. MEREDITH *(Rising):* Why, the very idea! I've never been so insulted in my life. *(She sits.)*

THOMPSON: Just answer the question, Miss Bedford.

WILLARD *(To* ALICE): Did Mr. Brier tell you that he was changing his will?

ALICE: Yes. He asked Clay to go to town that afternoon and return with his lawyer.

WILLARD: What afternoon was that?

ALICE: The afternoon Mr. Brier was—*(Upset)* the afternoon he died.

WILLARD: And who were the beneficiaries of the new will?

ALICE: Mr. Brier didn't live to make a new will.

WILLARD: Very convenient for the present heirs. Remember, Miss Bedford, you're under oath. Who are Mr. Brier's heirs in the present will?

ALICE: Mr. Brier's entire estate is divided equally among Bruce Collins, his nephew, Everett Franklin, Mr. Brier's friend, and—Clay Trevor.

WILLARD: Was the estate a substantial one?

ALICE: Mr. Brier's estate was valued at several million dollars.

WILLARD: And did Mr. Brier indicate to you how he planned to change his will?

ALICE: No. I knew nothing about that.

WILLARD: Is it possible that he was planning to exclude one or more of the original beneficiaries from the new will?

ALICE: I—I don't know.

WILLARD *(Insistently):* Isn't it possible that he was planning to exclude Clay Trevor from his will?

ALICE: No, no! (CLAY *rises and rushes up to* WILLARD.)

CLAY: Why don't you ask *me* that question? Why are you persecuting Alice? I tell you, she had nothing to do with it. Mr. Brier was going to exclude me from his new will— at my request! (JURORS *and* SPECTATORS *whisper.* SHANNON *rises.* THOMPSON *pounds gavel.*)

SHANNON: Your Honor, I object!

THOMPSON: Sustained. We will have no more outbursts in this courtroom. (*To* CLAY) Does the defendant realize the seriousness of his statement?

CLAY: Of course I do. I asked Mr. Brier to exclude me from his will so that I could try to make it on my own. I was going to leave Parrot Island, and I didn't want his help—I wanted to prove something to myself.

WILLARD (*Sarcastically*): A noble gesture. (*Coldly*) Isn't it true that when you found out he was planning to cut you out of his will, you killed him before a new will could be drawn up?

CLAY: That's a lie! (*He raises his fist.* SHANNON *quickly restrains him, pulls him back to defense table. They sit.*)

WILLARD: I think Mr. Trevor's admission speaks for itself. I have no further questions. (MISS NETTLETON *raises her hand.* WILLARD *glares at her, then explodes.*) Miss Nettleton, you're out of order!

MISS NETTLETON: Nonsense, young man. I've never felt better in my life. (*To* ALICE) My dear, you mentioned that the estate was divided equally among three men.

ALICE (*Nodding*): Clay Trevor, Bruce Collins, and Everett Franklin.

MISS NETTLETON: Well, I know how people like to gossip in our little community, and isn't it possible that Mr. Collins or Everett Franklin might have learned that Alexander Brier was planning to change his will? After all, Mr. Brier might have planned to exclude either of them, too. I think that any of the gentlemen in the old will might have had a reason to kill Mr. Brier.

MRS. PITNEY: Why, sure! Bruce Collins or Everett Franklin might have killed Brier as easily as Clay Trevor could. (FRANKLIN *coughs uneasily.*)

WILLARD: Objection!

THOMPSON: Objection sustained. (*To* CLERK) Strike those statements from the record. (*Turns*) Miss Nettleton, please try to refrain from further outbursts.

MISS NETTLETON (*Sadly*): It was just a thought. (*She resumes knitting.*)

WILLARD: The State calls its next witness, Mr. Bruce Collins. (ALICE *steps down;* COLLINS *leaves his seat in the audience, takes oath, sits in witness box.*) You are Bruce Collins, Alexander Brier's nephew, correct?

COLLINS: That's right.

WILLARD: And you live in the house on Parrot Island?

COLLINS: Only during the summer. My work—and my apartment—are in New York.

WILLARD: Were you in Alexander Brier's house on July 28th?

COLLINS: I was there in the morning. I left for Lockwood right after lunch, a little before one.

WILLARD: Did you take the causeway?

COLLINS: Yes. I don't like to sail, and though it's longer, I drove.

WILLARD: Did you pass any other cars?

COLLINS: No, sir. I didn't see another car until I reached Lockwood.

WILLARD: Who was at the house when you left?

COLLINS: The maid, the housekeeper, and Miss Bedford. And Clay, of course.

WILLARD: Clay Trevor remained at the house?

COLLINS: Yes. My uncle wanted him to do an errand that afternoon.

WILLARD: What errand?

COLLINS: He wanted Clay to drive to Lockwood and pick

up his lawyer at the bank. Then Clay was supposed to drive the lawyer back to the house.

WILLARD *(To* COLLINS): To your knowledge, did Clay Trevor go to the bank, as planned?

COLLINS: Yes. Both Clay and the lawyer were at the house when I came back later in the afternoon.

WILLARD: Thank you, Mr. Collins. *(To* SHANNON) Your witness. (SHANNON *rises and approaches witness stand.)*

SHANNON: Mr. Collins, is there anyone who can prove you were in Lockwood the afternoon of the murder?

COLLINS: Well, I went to a few shops, but I didn't meet anyone I knew. *(Angrily)* Why should I have to prove anything? I'm not on trial!

SHANNON: No one is on trial, Mr. Collins. We're just trying to establish some facts. I have no further questions. (SHANNON *sits.)*

WILLARD *(Sarcastically, to* MISS NETTLETON): Perhaps you'd like to question the witness, Miss Nettleton?

MISS NETTLETON: Oh, gracious, no! *(Slight pause)* But there is one little thing. *(She turns.)* Mr. Collins, did you know that your uncle was planning to change his will?

COLLINS: No! My uncle never informed me of his personal affairs.

MISS NETTLETON: But, as his nephew you must have expected to be a beneficiary in his present will, as Miss Bedford says you are.

COLLINS: Yes, I always thought that Uncle would include me. *(He crosses to seat in gallery. At the same time,* WILLARD *motions to* CLERK *who steps forward.)*

CLERK: Mrs. Vera Potts will take the stand. (MRS. POTTS *takes oath and sits in witness stand. She adjusts her glasses.)*

WILLARD: Mrs. Potts, you are employed as maid at the home of the late Alexander Brier, correct?

MRS. POTTS *(Haughtily):* I am a professional domestic at Parrot Island.

WILLARD: Do you recall the afternoon of July 28th?

MRS. POTTS: How can I ever forget it? Oh, poor Mr. Brier! I don't know how that dreadful Clay Trevor could have done such a thing.

SHANNON *(Rising quickly):* I object!

THOMPSON: Objection sustained. The witness will not express her opinions at this hearing.

MRS. POTTS: Well, I saw him with my own eyes.

WILLARD *(Quickly):* Exactly *what* did you see, Mrs. Potts?

MRS. POTTS *(Importantly):* I was in the kitchen, cleaning up after lunch. It was just one o'clock.

WILLARD: How can you be so certain of the time?

MRS. POTTS: While I do the dishes, I always watch my favorite daytime serials. I had just seen *Frieda Faces Life.* What a program! Poor Frieda can't decide whether to marry a wealthy British nobleman or the handsome, young captain from the Swiss Navy.

WILLARD: Mrs. Potts, please!

MRS. POTTS *(Defensively):* I was only trying to set the time. Frieda's program ends at one o'clock and I was waiting to see *Valiant Valerie. (Gushing)* You really should watch *Valiant Valerie* sometime.

WILLARD *(Impatiently):* Will you please continue with your testimony?

MRS. POTTS: The theme music for *Valiant Valerie* had just begun when I saw him running across the back lawn.

WILLARD *(Quickly):* Whom did you see?

MRS. POTTS: Mr. Trevor, of course! He came from the far side of the house, from the direction of the library, and ran down to the boathouse.

WILLARD: Are you certain that the man you saw was Mr. Trevor?

MRS. POTTS: I don't understand why you keep asking me that. I guess I know Mr. Trevor when I see him!

WILLARD *(To* THOMPSON): Sergeant Tolliver testified that he received the call from Parrot Island at 1:10, just ten minutes after Mrs. Potts saw Clay Trevor running from the library. I have no further questions. (*He gestures at* SHANNON) Your witness. (SHANNON *rises, walks to witness box.*)

SHANNON: Mrs. Potts, I am sure that you are aware of the importance of your testimony.

MRS. POTTS: Indeed I am.

SHANNON: Did the man you saw running pass close to the kitchen window?

MRS. POTTS: Well, not exactly. You see, there is a terrace outside the window, and the man was on the other side of the terrace.

SHANNON (*To* THOMPSON): Your Honor, we have measured the distance from the kitchen window to the terrace approach to the boathouse. It's more than three hundred and fifty feet. It would be impossible to make a positive identification from that distance.

MRS. POTTS: I know what I saw. It was Clay Trevor, wearing the same green sweater that he always wore around the house.

SHANNON: But isn't it a fact, Mrs. Potts, that you are identifying a sweater rather than a man!

MRS. POTTS (*Ruffled*): Well, I saw him. I'm sure of that.

MISS NETTLETON (*Rising*): Vera, when was the last time you had your eyes examined?

THOMPSON (*Angrily*): Really, Miss Nettleton, we cannot tolerate these frequent interruptions.

MRS. POTTS (*Ignoring him*): I can't rightly remember, Amanda—but my eyesight's as good as yours.

MISS NETTLETON: Vera, what color is this sweater? (*She holds up her knitting.* MRS. POTTS *squints, adjusts her glasses.*)

MRS. POTTS: Anybody can see it's green. (JURORS *and* SPECTATORS *whisper excitedly.*)

MISS NETTLETON: You're sure?

MRS. POTTS (*Nodding*): As green as they come!

MISS NETTLETON: Vera, this is a blue sweater. Green would

look positively horrible on Hannah's boy. It wouldn't suit him at all.

SHANNON *(Happily):* Your Honor, we have no further questions.

THOMPSON: Step down, Mrs. Potts. (MRS. POTTS *crosses to* MISS NETTLETON, *looks again at sweater, then returns to her seat in gallery.* WILLARD *rises.*)

WILLARD: I call my final witness, Mrs. Meredith. (MRS. MEREDITH, *a thin, nervous woman, takes the oath and sits in witness box.*) Your name is Mrs. Ella Meredith?

MRS. MEREDITH: That's right. *(She pulls at collar of her dress.)*

WILLARD: There is no need to be nervous, Mrs. Meredith. Just answer my questions. Were you employed by the late Alexander Brier?

MRS. MEREDITH: I was his housekeeper.

WILLARD: How long did you hold the position?

MRS. MEREDITH: Fifteen years.

WILLARD: And were you working on the afternoon of July 28th?

MRS. MEREDITH: Yes, sir.

WILLARD: Will you tell us what happened that afternoon?

MRS. MEREDITH: Mr. Brier had lunch on the patio outside the library, with his nephew and Mr. Trevor.

WILLARD: What happened then?

MRS. MEREDITH: After lunch, Mr. Collins took his car and drove to Lockwood.

SHANNON *(Rising):* I object! The allegation that Mr. Collins drove to Lockwood is an assumption on the part of the witness.

THOMPSON: Objection sustained.

WILLARD *(Impatiently):* Will you continue, Mrs. Meredith, and confine your testimony to answering my questions?

MRS. MEREDITH *(Nervously):* I only know what Mr. Collins told me.

WILLARD: Did you know how Mr. Trevor planned to spend the afternoon?

MRS. MEREDITH *(Nodding):* Mr. Brier told Mr. Trevor to pick up his lawyer at the bank. Mr. Brier spoke those very words at the luncheon table.

WILLARD: What happened after lunch?

MRS. MEREDITH: Mrs. Potts cleared away the dishes and took them to the kitchen. Mr. Brier left the patio and went into the library. He was expecting Mr. Franklin.

WILLARD: What time was that?

MRS. MEREDITH: It was about ten minutes to one.

WILLARD: Did you remain on the patio?

MRS. MEREDITH: No, I went to speak to the gardener, who was working on the other side of the house.

WILLARD: Did you see Mr. Trevor after lunch?

MRS. MEREDITH: No. I figured that he went to the garage to get the car for the trip to the bank.

WILLARD: What did you do then?

MRS. MEREDITH: The gardener and I had gone to the front of the house, when I heard something that sounded like backfire, or a shot. I was frightened, and I thought the sound came from the garage at first. Then I realized that it had come from inside the house, so I hurried in, looked in the library, and found—*(Her voice breaks off.)*

WILLARD: I realize the strain of these past weeks, Mrs. Meredith, but it is imperative that we have your testimony. What did you find in the library?

MRS. MEREDITH: I found Mr. Brier lying on the floor, near his desk. *(Shaking head)* But he wasn't dead when I found him. Mr. Brier was still alive! (JURORS *and* SPECTATORS *talk excitedly.* THOMPSON *raps for order.)* I reached for the phone to call a doctor, but he grabbed my arm. *(Tearfully)* He—he knew that there was nothing I could do for him. *(Her fingers tighten around her left arm.)* And—and then he spoke to me.

WILLARD: Did Mr. Brier name his attacker?

MRS. MEREDITH: It—it was difficult to understand him. I

heard him whisper: "The bank—he's gone to the bank. Stop him." *(She sobs.)*

WILLARD: He mentioned the bank?

MRS. MEREDITH: Those were Mr. Brier's words. And then he finally said: "Don't let him get away. He did this to me." *(More sobs. Loud talking in gallery.* SHANNON *looks at* CLAY. THOMPSON *pounds gavel, restores order.)*

WILLARD: And, to the best of your knowledge, there was only one member of the household who went to the bank that afternoon.

MRS. MEREDITH: Yes—that person was Clay Trevor! (MISS NETTLETON *raises her hand.)*

WILLARD *(Angrily):* Miss Nettleton, in view of the testimony just offered, I feel this is hardly the time for an interruption.

THOMPSON: I am inclined to agree with Mr. Willard. Is there a question you would like to direct to the court to clarify Mrs. Meredith's testimony?

MISS NETTLETON: I really don't think it was any testimony at all. Mr. Brier's dying words don't necessarily point to Mr. Trevor as the murderer.

WILLARD *(Impatiently):* Three witnesses have testified to Mr. Trevor's proposed trip to the bank on the afternoon of July 28th. We know Mr. Trevor made the trip because he returned to the house with Mr. Brier's lawyer.

MISS NETTLETON: Precisely. Everyone knows that Mr. Trevor went to the bank to get the lawyer, but don't you think Mr. Brier's final words were a trifle odd?

WILLARD: Odd?

MISS NETTLETON: Of course! Why didn't Mr. Brier say that Clay was at the lawyer's? Better still, why didn't he mention Clay by name?

MRS. MEREDITH: I told you what Mr. Brier said. It's the truth!

MISS NETTLETON: Oh, we're not doubting your testimony, Ella. You've been repeating too many conversations for years to miss a single word! (*Murmurs and scattered laughter from* SPECTATORS.)

WILLARD (*Insistently*): Your Honor, the fact remains that Mr. Brier mentioned the bank and, by the testimony of all concerned parties, Mr. Trevor was the only person involved who went to the bank that afternoon.

MISS NETTLETON (*Calmly*): Jeff Willard, you're still as impetuous as you were back in high school. (*Slowly*) There was another person at the bank that afternoon, and we've been insufferable fools not to realize it. If it pleases the court—I believe that's the phrase—I'd like to ask Sergeant John Tolliver a question.

WILLARD: This is an outrage!

THOMPSON: Miss Nettleton's request is unusual, indeed, but since this is a preliminary hearing, I will grant her request. Call Sergeant Tolliver to the witness stand.

CLERK: Sergeant Tolliver to the witness stand. (TOLLIVER *crosses to witness stand as* MRS. MEREDITH *steps down.*)

MISS NETTLETON: John, you traveled to Parrot Island by boat from Sands Crossing?

TOLLIVER: That's right, Miss Nettleton.

MISS NETTLETON: And you mentioned that you saw Everett Franklin as you approached the island?

TOLLIVER (*Nodding*): We arrived at the same time. Mr. Franklin came up to the house with us.

MISS NETTLETON: And where did you leave the police launch, John?

TOLLIVER (*Smiling faintly*): Why, we moored our launch with Mr. Franklin's boat at the bank—but I don't see. . . . (*Suddenly*) The bank!

MISS NETTLETON: Yes, John. The bank again. (*To* THOMPSON) Really, Your Honor, the English language can be so confusing at times.

WILLARD (*Impatiently*): This is hardly the time for a lesson in grammar.

MISS NETTLETON: You were never very good in grammar,

JEFF. You should have paid attention when we studied homonyms. (*To* THOMPSON) You see, Amos—Your Honor—Clay Trevor wasn't the only person at the bank that afternoon. Sergeant Tolliver was there—and Everett Franklin was there, too!

FRANKLIN (*Standing*): Miss Nettleton, I don't like your insinuation!

MISS NETTLETON: I meant no offense. Why, anyone could build a case against John Tolliver—or you!—out of the evidence. Let's suppose that you arrived at Alexander Brier's house immediately after lunch. You might have joined him in the library without being seen by anyone in the household.

FRANKLIN: Preposterous!

MISS NETTLETON: Not at all, Mr. Franklin. You might have learned that Mr. Brier was planning to change his will. Isn't it possible that he was planning to cut you out of the will—and not Clay Trevor?

FRANKLIN: I demand the immediate dismissal of this woman as a member of the jury!

MISS NETTLETON: But I'm simply trying to show you how a case can be built against anyone. After you shot Mr. Brier with Clay Trevor's gun—a gun that you knew was always kept in the library desk—you ran to Trevor's bedroom and planted the gun in his closet. You then left by the French doors in the library, and rounded the house, where you were seen by Mrs. Potts. Remember, she identified a sweater—not a man. Then you returned to your boat—moored at the bank!

FRANKLIN: Ridiculous!

MISS NETTLETON: You headed out into the bay and, when you saw the police launch approaching, you returned to the bank and joined John Tolliver. The sergeant thought you were just arriving at Parrot Island but, actually, you were leaving! (*To* MRS. MEREDITH) What were Mr. Brier's final words?

MRS. MEREDITH *(Slowly):* "The bank—he's gone to the bank. Stop him. Don't let him get away. He did this to me."

MISS NETTLETON: Yes, Mr. Brier's murderer escaped to the bank, and Mr. Brier knew that you came to Parrot Island by boat. I'm afraid, Mr. Franklin, that Mr. Brier's words fit you very well. *(SPECTATORS whisper together. THOMPSON raps for order. MISS NETTLETON turns to TOLLIVER.)* Sergeant, do you remember what Mr. Franklin was wearing that afternoon?

TOLLIVER *(Rubbing forehead):* Well, I guess he was wearing sport clothes. Maybe a jacket. *(Slowly)* No! He was wearing a sweater. A blue sweater!

MISS NETTLETON *(Nodding):* Mrs. Potts saw a man in a green sweater—but we know she's color blind, and sees blue as green. *(Relentlessly)* And it would be easy to call the marine base where you moor your boat, to find the exact time you sailed on the 28th. They keep a log of all arrivals and departures.

FRANKLIN *(Furiously):* This is absurd!

MISS NETTLETON: It might prove that Everett Franklin sailed much earlier than we imagined. It might prove that he had ample time to kill Mr. Brier before the police arrived! *(MRS. POTTS stands, squints at FRANKLIN, and nods emphatically.)*

MRS. POTTS: I believe Amanda could be right. Yes, Mr. Franklin could have been the man I saw running toward the bank. *(All turn to FRANKLIN, who sags against table, wipes his brow.)*

FRANKLIN *(Weakly):* He told me he was changing his will—cutting me out without a penny. After all these years—I don't know, somehow I had the gun in my hand. I didn't mean to kill him, I didn't want to—but then I had to get away. I ran upstairs and hid the gun in Trevor's closet, then I went downstairs and into the library again. Brier kept staring at me as I crossed the room and ran out the door. I—I think he called my name. He knew I was heading for my boat, at the bank. *(Brokenly)* Yes, I killed him.

THOMPSON: Sergeant Tolliver, take Mr. Franklin into custody. (SERGEANT TOLLIVER *crosses to* FRANKLIN, *leads him off.*) This hearing is closed. Mr. Trevor, no charges will be filed against you. (ALICE BEDFORD *rushes to* CLAY *and they embrace.*)

ALICE: Oh, Clay, I knew they were wrong to suspect you. I knew it!

CLAY: Alice, I—

ALICE: Don't talk about it. Don't think about anything but the future. *(He smiles, and they exit together.)*

MRS. SHAW: Amanda, you're simply the limit.

MRS. PITNEY: She probably suspected Franklin all the time.

MISS NETTLETON: It was nothing. (JURORS *and* SPECTATORS *file out slowly, talking among themselves.*) You know, it's really amazing what will happen when a body puts her mind to thinking.

WILLARD: Miss Nettleton, I don't know how you did it, but I'm going to put my mind to thinking, too!

MISS NETTLETON: Willard, you leave me only one more thing to say. *(She pounds on rail of jury box, smiles).* Case dismissed! *(Curtain)*

THE END

Production Notes

The Sixth Juror

Characters: 8 male; 6 female; 9 male and female extras for Other Jurors, and as many as desired for Spectators.

Playing Time: 35 minutes.

Costumes: Everyday dress. Judge wears a long black robe.

Properties: Shapeless blue knitting for Miss Nettleton; stenotype machine for Clerk; gavel for Judge; gun with tag.

Setting: Courtroom in Sands Crossing courthouse. Judge's bench is up center, with Clerk's table in front of it. Witness stand is up right, and jury box is at extreme right, at an angle to face audience. Defense counsel's table and prosecutor's table are left and right, at an angle and facing audience. Spectators' gallery is down left.

Lighting: No special effects.

The Door

Characters

NURSE WITHERS
MRS. MERLIN
PAUL MERLIN

SETTING: *The living room of the Merlin cottage. Up center is entranceway leading to hall and kitchen. A working door leading to Paul Merlin's room is left.*

AT RISE: MRS. MERLIN, *a pale, thin woman, and* NURSE WITHERS, *a young woman in white uniform, are seated in living room.* MRS. MERLIN *sits quietly, but* NURSE WITHERS *is plainly nervous. The clock strikes five.*

MRS. MERLIN: I must get Paul's tea tray ready. He's very particular about such things.

NURSE: May I help you? *(She jumps up nervously.)*

MRS. MERLIN: Not now, thank you, Miss Withers. *(She fingers beads she wears.)* You will have plenty of work to do shortly. Meanwhile, I want you to get used to our little house.

NURSE *(Smiling):* I know my job, Mrs. Merlin. I can't understand why you refuse to let me help my patient. You know I've had lots of experience at the State Hospital and in private homes.

MRS. MERLIN: But Paul is not really a problem. We've been married for twenty-five years, and—well, I can't imagine what he'll do when I go.

NURSE: Nonsense, Mrs. Merlin! You have many years ahead. I usually have a case dumped in my lap as soon as I reach a house, but I've been here for almost twenty-four hours and haven't met Mr. Merlin yet.

MRS. MERLIN: You will meet Paul in good time. Have no fear of that! Furthermore, you must be tired after that dreadful journey last night.

NURSE: It's true. I'm not used to Maine coast thunderstorms. And with no cab at the railroad station, I had that long walk up to this house. *(Shakes her head)* I've never walked more than seven city blocks at one time in my life! Thank heavens I sent my trunk by express.

MRS. MERLIN: You poor dear! I hope you will be comfortable in our house.

NURSE: Who wouldn't be comfortable in such a charming place!

MRS. MERLIN: Oh, not everyone has been. There have been other nurses, you know.

NURSE: Other nurses?

MRS. MERLIN: Yes. Remember, I told you that Paul is—difficult. But he's all I have left. I've catered to his every whim for ten years, and there are many things—well, it is not easy for one to understand.

NURSE: I'm afraid you don't trust nurses. We really are a capable lot.

MRS. MERLIN: You do seem very kind, and I shall entrust Paul to your care in a few days.

NURSE: A few days! I thought my duties were required immediately.

MRS. MERLIN *(Quickly)*: As long as I remain in this house, I will attend to Paul.

NURSE *(Angrily)*: Mrs. Merlin, I assure you I am capable of carrying out my duties. If you doubt my capability, I am sure that the nurses' registry can send someone else.

MRS. MERLIN *(Quickly)*: You mustn't go, Miss Withers.

Please, please, have patience. Leave Paul to me—for a little while at least.

NURSE *(Slowly):* For a little while? I don't understand—

MRS. MERLIN *(Vaguely):* You will soon.

NURSE *(Briskly):* What is the nature of Mr. Merlin's injury?

MRS. MERLIN: It was an automobile accident. Now, let me see. It happened ten years ago this very day!

NURSE: Doesn't he leave his room?

MRS. MERLIN: Only on rare occasions. His left leg is paralyzed, and he has difficulty using his cane.

NURSE: He must be very lonesome in there. Why doesn't he join us?

MRS. MERLIN: Paul finds comfort in his solitude. He always liked people, but since his accident, he seems to live in another world.

NURSE: Alone in a room for ten years! The poor man surely needs some diversion.

MRS. MERLIN: Paul is not lonesome. Our love is very strong. *(Breaks off)* But perhaps you think I am a sentimental old woman.

NURSE: No, no, I can imagine how you feel.

MRS. MERLIN: Paul's confinement has brought us closer together. Before the accident, he was always hurrying off on business trips, or when he was home, we had lots of parties and long, boring card games. *(Sadly)* Friends never come to our house any more.

NURSE: Do you know how *he* feels about his situation?

MRS. MERLIN: Paul is a hollow shell since the accident. He frightens me at times. But then we *are* together, and that is a great compensation. (NURSE *looks puzzled.*) Now, Miss Withers, don't look at me so strangely. Perhaps I am a selfish woman, but I won't let anyone take Paul away from me!

NURSE *(Bitterly):* If you have managed so nicely for ten years, why do you suddenly need a nurse?

MRS. MERLIN: That is a difficult question to answer. *(Pause)*
There is no explanation. *(Slowly)* You will find out for
yourself.

NURSE: But I want to get on with my work. I'll get lazy
without something to do!

MRS. MERLIN: You will find much to do—later.

NURSE *(Hesitantly):* I don't know whether I want to stay on
this case.

MRS. MERLIN *(Pleading):* Do say that you will stay, Miss
Withers!

NURSE *(Reluctantly):* All right. I'll try it anyway.

MRS. MERLIN: Thank you, my dear. *(Pauses briefly)* But I
mustn't delay any longer. Paul's tea tray is past due. If
you will excuse me—*(Stands)*

NURSE: May I take the tray to Mr. Merlin?

MRS. MERLIN: Oh, no; just rest and make yourself comfortable. I want Paul to get used to the idea of another
nurse in the house.

NURSE: What does he do all day? I haven't heard him once.

MRS. MERLIN: He sits in bed, propped against the pillows,
and watches the sea. Listen! Can you hear the sea? My
Paul loves the sea.

NURSE: It frightens me. I imagine this house is lovely in
the summer, but how do you manage during the winter
months?

MRS. MERLIN: We don't mind the seasons or the treacher-
ous weather of winter. The earth is a thing of beauty to
Paul and me. We feel quite secure in our little cliff house
overlooking the sea. *(Slowly, MRS. MERLIN crosses to hall
entrance and goes into kitchen. NURSE is plainly nervous. She
walks back and forth, stares at PAUL's door and shudders. Then
she starts for kitchen but stops short, stands in front of fireplace
and grandfather clock. A rumble of thunder is heard, and she
gasps in terror. Presently, she walks over to a magazine rack
beside bay window, picks up two magazines and returns to her
chair. She leafs through magazines and stops abruptly.)*

NURSE *(Nervously)*: Why, these magazines are ten years old! And the pages have never been opened! *(She shudders, and drops one of the magazines.)* Time has stood still in this house for ten years! *(Frightened)* And what about Mr. Merlin in that room? I have to know. I have to know! *(She leaves her chair and rushes toward door of* PAUL's *room as* MRS. MERLIN, *tea tray balanced in one hand, re-enters.)*

MRS. MERLIN *(Sharply)*: Don't go in now. I wouldn't want to upset Paul before tea.

NURSE *(Upset)*: I—I'm sorry. The silence of this house got on my nerves, and for a moment, I imagined—

MRS. MERLIN *(Quickly)*: What did you imagine?

NURSE: Oh, it's foolish, I know, but Mr. Merlin's accident— your devotion—these old magazines. It seems as though time stands still in this house.

MRS. MERLIN: Time is meaningless. *(With her free hand,* MRS. MERLIN *reaches into pocket of her dress, takes out bunch of keys, walks to* PAUL's *door.* NURSE *looks on, in fascination.)*

NURSE: What are you doing?

MRS. MERLIN: Why, unlocking the door, of course.

NURSE: You keep Mr. Merlin locked in his room?

MRS. MERLIN: Paul prefers it that way.

NURSE: I don't understand.

MRS. MERLIN: Paul insists upon privacy!

NURSE: I don't believe any man would want to be kept prisoner in his own house!

MRS. MERLIN: Paul isn't like any other man.

NURSE: You must let me see my patient—tonight.

MRS. MERLIN: Only with Paul's permission.

NURSE *(Almost hysterical)*: Permission or not, I insist.

MRS. MERLIN *(Firmly)*: Miss Withers, you must have faith in me. You must help me.

NURSE: Help?

MRS. MERLIN: I suppose I have seemed rude, but please, can't you trust me for a little while longer?

NURSE: But there are so many things I don't understand. Why can't I meet my patient?

MRS. MERLIN: You will, you will, but don't deprive me of these few moments alone with Paul. There is so little time left.

NURSE *(Sharply):* Mrs. Merlin, why are you afraid of me?

MRS. MERLIN *(Nervously):* I am not afraid, my dear.

NURSE: I am here to help your husband, but you won't let me. Why are you keeping me away?

MRS. MERLIN *(Sadly):* You will know shortly. You can't realize how happy I've been these last few days with Paul. It's been a new life—a rebirth of everything fine and good in our marriage. For the first time in twenty-five years, I feel that Paul loves me. Don't take that away from me. *(Bewildered,* NURSE *retreats two steps, staring at* MRS. MERLIN.) You think I am mad, don't you? You think that Paul's accident has affected my mind and that I am a depraved old lady. You may be right, but I am not as mean as you think. It has not been my selfishness that keeps Paul a prisoner in that room. *(Abruptly)* Heavens! Paul's tea is getting cold! Please excuse me. (MRS. MERLIN *quickly unlocks door of* PAUL's *room and pauses, smiling, on the threshold. As if speaking to someone in* PAUL's *room.)* Here's your tea, Paul. And how are you this afternoon? *(She enters* PAUL's *room, closing door behind her.* NURSE *backs away from door and returns to her chair, where she perches nervously on the edge of seat, her eyes riveted on* PAUL's *door. After a pause, knob turns, and door swings open.* MRS. MERLIN *emerges slowly, sighing heavily as she turns to close door. Glancing at* NURSE, *she quickly reaches into pocket for keys and locks door.)* I told Paul all about you. He's quite eager to meet you.

NURSE *(Coldly):* I didn't hear you talking to anyone in that room.

MRS. MERLIN: The walls are very thick, and Paul's voice is very weak.

NURSE: Who—what is in that room?

MRS. MERLIN: Miss Withers, please—not yet!

NURSE: I must know! I can't stand this madness any longer.

MRS. MERLIN: You will know. Paul will see you tonight.

NURSE *(Slowly, in frightened voice):* I don't know whether I can go into that room.

MRS. MERLIN: Why not?

NURSE *(Slowly):* I don't know what I will find behind that locked door.

MRS. MERLIN: You will find a sick, tired old man who needs help. You mustn't deny him that help. He's all alone.

NURSE *(Coldly):* You seem quite capable of managing on your own.

MRS. MERLIN: That's unkind, Miss Withers. Don't you realize I want to stay with Paul forever?

NURSE *(Firmly):* Well, you can stay alone. I'm leaving this house tonight! And there's nothing you can do to stop me!

MRS. MERLIN *(Sadly):* No. I can't stop you. *(Brightly)* But at least stay for supper. Maybe we can talk this out after you have relaxed.

NURSE: Very well. But I don't intend to stay in this house tonight.

MRS. MERLIN: Perhaps you'll change your mind. After you have met Paul, you might change your mind about many things. (MRS. MERLIN *walks toward kitchen, carrying tea tray, and exits.* NURSE *remains seated. She looks at* PAUL'S *door, rises and walks toward doorway of kitchen.*)

NURSE *(Calling):* Mrs. Merlin! *(She looks into kitchen.)* Mrs. Merlin! *(She turns and crosses to bay window.)* Where could she be? Has she left me alone in this dreadful house? (NURSE *rushes off. Loud pounding is heard. In a moment,* NURSE *returns, obviously agitated.*) She's locked me in! Locked in with that—that whatever-it-is behind the door! *(She sobs uncontrollably. Finally, she strides to* PAUL'S *door, pauses, then calls softly.)* Mr. Merlin? *(A trifle louder)* Mr. Merlin. Can you hear me? *(Her hand raps gently on the door, then tries to turn the knob but it won't turn.)* Mr. Merlin! Why don't you answer me? You are there in that room, aren't you? Please answer me! *(Hysterically)* Mr. Merlin! Why did your wife leave me alone? What's going on here? *(She pauses, but no sound is heard.)* I know that you're still alive, Mr. Merlin. Mrs. Merlin thinks that you're dead, but you're alive. You have to be alive! *(She sinks into her chair, sobbing.)* There must be a man in that room. He can't be dead! (MRS. MERLIN *silently enters.*)

MRS. MERLIN: No, he isn't dead. My Paul will never die. (NURSE *spins around and sees* MRS. MERLIN *standing behind her.*)

NURSE: Where—where were you?

MRS. MERLIN: I had a few things to do.

NURSE: Why did you leave me alone?

MRS. MERLIN: You were not alone. Paul was with you. Paul will always be with you. (NURSE *turns, points to entranceway.*)

NURSE: Open the front door at once! Why did you lock me in?

MRS. MERLIN: I didn't want you to leave before we finished our little talk.

NURSE: You're mad—insane! I want to leave at once! (MRS. MERLIN *extends her hand to* NURSE.)

MRS. MERLIN: Miss Withers, I implore you to stay. Paul is not difficult to manage. You will love him—wait for his every call—be at hand any time of the day or night he needs you. You cannot leave Paul now. It is too late to do anything about it.

NURSE *(Frightened):* Too late?

MRS. MERLIN: Yes, too late for many things. (NURSE *starts toward exit, but* MRS. MERLIN *blocks the way.*) Sit down. (NURSE *sits.*) There, that is better, my dear. Relax now, Miss Withers, and listen to what I must say.

NURSE *(Quickly):* I don't want to hear about it. I just want to leave this house.

MRS. MERLIN *(Sternly):* I will tell you why I brought you to this house. After that, you may leave if you please. But I think you will stay, Miss Withers. You see, you're going to meet Paul in a little while. (NURSE *glances toward door of* PAUL*'s room and recoils in terror.* MRS. MERLIN *watches her, smiles.*) Don't look so alarmed. After all, you wanted to meet Paul. You told me that you insisted upon visiting your patient tonight. I will grant you that wish.

NURSE *(Beseechingly):* Please don't torture me. Where did you go a little while ago? Why is Mr. Merlin's room locked? Why does time stand still in this house? Why is everything so—so—

MRS. MERLIN: So strange?

NURSE *(Frantically):* I don't know! I don't know! Something is terribly wrong in this house.

MRS. MERLIN *(Indignantly):* Nothing is wrong in my house. Haven't I cared for Paul all these years? Many people have tried to take him away, but he is mine, I tell you, he is mine! (MRS. MERLIN *controls herself and continues.*) But, before you go to Paul, I must tell you about his accident.

NURSE *(Desperately):* Please do!

MRS. MERLIN *(Composed):* Before the accident ten years ago, we had been very happy—Paul and I. We had many friends in town! People were always dropping in to visit us. And Paul loved to play bridge! We were returning from a bridge game the night he was taken away from me.

NURSE: Taken away—what do you mean?

MRS. MERLIN: The road was particularly bad that night. We turned at the intersection but Paul couldn't control the car. We crashed—overturned. The car was afire!

NURSE: Please—don't talk about it.

MRS. MERLIN *(Continuing, as if not hearing her):* We were taken to the hospital. It was very late.

NURSE: Were you in the hospital for a long time?

MRS. MERLIN *(Smiling):* No, my dear. I stayed there a very short time. I didn't worry about myself. I thought only of Paul. It's been that way ever since. That crash took

Paul away from me. Yes, these ten years have been very long.

NURSE: Ten years ago! That is the date of those magazines! Ten years ago! *(Her voice breaks off.)*

MRS. MERLIN: The accident did strange, horrible things to us. That is why I wanted you to get used to our house. No one else has stayed. No one loves Paul as I do, you see. Say that you will stay, Miss Withers. I—Paul needs you. Oh, it's not what you think. It's not what you think!

NURSE: What can I think? What is in that room?

MRS. MERLIN: Soon, you will know. And now, before you meet Paul, I want you to look in the Bible by the clock. (NURSE *turns and faces clock. She notices a small table near the clock, on which rests a small, voluminous Bible. Like a robot,* NURSE *crosses room, lifts Bible, and leafs through pages, finding a bulky object between the pages. She replaces Bible on table and unwraps package, takes out object. It is a black, silk sash. Inscribed in gold-block letters is the name:* MERLIN. *She stares at the letter on sash, then lets it fall to floor.)*

NURSE *(Screaming):* A funeral sash! He's dead! He's dead!

(MRS. MERLIN *fingers her key ring and unlocks* PAUL's *door.)*

MRS. MERLIN *(Calling):* Paul! Paul! Miss Withers is waiting to see you.

NURSE: He's dead! (MRS. MERLIN *steps back, still holding the key ring.)*

MRS. MERLIN: Goodbye, Miss Withers. And please try to understand. (NURSE *turns but finds that* MRS. MERLIN *has gone. She trembles, takes a step forward toward* PAUL's *door and stops abruptly. Doorknob is turning slowly. She hears the catch sliding back; door opens slowly.* PAUL MERLIN *appears. He is a bent, white-haired old man, gripping a cane. He wears faded gray dressing gown. He approaches* NURSE *and tries to smile.)*

PAUL: Miss Withers?

NURSE *(Terrified):* Yes.

PAUL: Agatha told me to expect you this evening.

NURSE: Agatha?

PAUL: Yes. Mrs. Merlin. (NURSE, *sobbing, steps toward* PAUL MERLIN.)

NURSE: You are alive!

PAUL: There, there, my child.

NURSE: I—I—Mr. Merlin—

PAUL: Don't be frightened. The other nurses were all frightened, but there's nothing really alarming about a feeble old man.

NURSE: I didn't know what to expect.

PAUL: Mrs. Merlin has upset you. But you mustn't mind Agatha. She means well, but there are people who don't understand.

NURSE: She said that you were taken away from her.

PAUL: Yes, in a way, we were separated, and, although she has been called away tonight, I don't think we'll ever really be apart.

NURSE *(Quickly):* She can't leave tonight. I'm not going to stay in this house!

PAUL: Are you still frightened? But soon you will come to love this house. I never wish to leave. I am alone here with my thoughts and the roar of the sea. Listen, do you hear the sea? (*He pauses briefly, his eyes focused sharply upon* NURSE.) The sea is like a voice calling me. Yes, you too will love the sea.

NURSE: Why did you stay locked in that room all these years?

PAUL: The other nurses treated me like a museum piece. I couldn't stand their prying eyes. Agatha saw that it wouldn't happen this time. Until she was ready—

NURSE: Ready? Ready for what?

PAUL: Please don't think about Agatha's strangeness anymore. All that is past, I assure you. But you must stay. You must stay!

NURSE: I will stay, but I will help Mrs. Merlin, too. She needs help!

PAUL: Help—for Agatha?

NURSE: Her mind is distorted since your accident. *(Quickly)* I understand so much now. The shock was too great for her. All these years of care have made her think of you as a ghost of the man she loved. Mr. Merlin, your wife thinks you are dead! We must help her! (PAUL MERLIN *looks at* NURSE *incredulously.*)

PAUL: You don't understand at all. *(Slowly)* Miss Withers, don't you know? Haven't you guessed?

NURSE *(Frightened):* What should I know?

PAUL: Did Agatha tell you everything about the accident?

NURSE: Yes. It happened ten years ago.

PAUL: It was a frightening experience. It happened like a lightning flash. Yes, I suppose I saw death for an instant. Death hovered close that night. Have you ever seen death, Miss Withers? *(She turns away.)* Death is not as intangible as one might think. Agatha is right in a way. I have lived with death for ten years. A death of loneliness and regrets. A living man can suffer death without knowing the horror of the grave. Do you realize what I am saying to you?

NURSE *(Completely unnerved):* No—no—I can't realize anything. I must be going mad.

PAUL: We were separated in that accident. I have been helpless in this house for many years.

NURSE: It's terrible—terrible!

PAUL: But my life was spared. I was not ready for death. (PAUL MERLIN's *voice trails off. Then, gripping his cane, he steps nearer* NURSE.) My wife was killed in the crash. (NURSE *looks at* PAUL MERLIN *in terror, as the curtain slowly falls.*)

THE END

Production Notes

The Door

Characters: 1 male; 2 female.

Playing Time: 25 minutes.

Costumes: Modern dress. Nurse Withers wears a white nurse's uniform. Mr. Merlin wears a faded gray dressing gown and carries a cane.

Properties: Tray with cup and saucer, ring of keys for Mrs. Merlin, black sash with gold letters spelling "Merlin" in Bible.

Setting: An attractively furnished living room in the Merlin cottage. Up center is a large entranceway to hall and kitchen. At right is a large fireplace, and near fireplace is old-fashioned grandfather clock. Next to clock is a small table on which rests a black Bible. A bay window is up left, and near it is a small magazine rack with magazines. Several comfortable chairs are at center. A working door to Paul Merlin's room is at left, angled so that it's visible to the audience.

Lighting: No special effects.

I Want to Report A Murder

Characters

HATTIE BARNES ⎫ *elderly sisters*
LOTTIE BARNES ⎭
MARY, *the Barnes's niece*
BARRY MORTON
ROD DANVERS
MR. GREGORY
KATIE, *a maid*
LIEUTENANT FLETCHER

TIME: *The present. Late afternoon.*
SETTING: *The living room in the Barnes home.*
AT RISE: *Stage is deserted.* LOTTIE BARNES *enters hurriedly at center, pauses, looks right and left, then crosses to left and looks out opening. Then, she quickly walks over to telephone table, raises phone, and dials a number.*
LOTTIE *(Into phone):* Hello. Police headquarters? I—I need your help. *(Pause)* Of course I want a policeman. Why do you think I called? *(Pause)* Yes, it is a real emergency. *(Quietly)* I want to report a murder! *(Pause)* Homicide department? Yes, yes. Let me speak to him! *(Pause)* Hello. Lieutenant Fletcher? *(Pause)* I called to report a murder! *(Pause)* I don't know *who's* been murdered. Someone's been killed—isn't that enough? (HATTIE BARNES, *her sister, enters center, hears* LOTTIE's *conversation.*) Really, Lieutenant! This is most exasperating! My name is Lottie Barnes, and I live with my sister, Hattie. *(Pause)*

Yes, the big, gray house on Maple Street. Well, we have several boarders—it was necessary after Father's death—and something very strange has happened. *(Pause)* Yes, Lieutenant, of course I'm going to tell you about the murder! (HATTIE *shakes her head, walks downstage quickly, takes phone from* LOTTIE *and hangs it up.*)

HATTIE: Really, Lottie! I'm surprised at you.

LOTTIE *(Defiantly):* I don't care! I told you I was going to call the police.

HATTIE: You're making a fool of yourself.

LOTTIE: I know what I'm doing, and you can't stop me, Hattie. I'm acting in your best interests.

HATTIE: *My* best interests? Good heavens, you'll drive the boarders out of our house. What are you trying to do?

LOTTIE: It's about Mr. Gregory, and you know it.

HATTIE *(Huffily):* Mr. Gregory is a fine old gentleman. His references were perfect. If he prefers to keep to himself, that's his business.

LOTTIE: You know that he's very—strange.

HATTIE: You'll be the death of me, Lottie! *(Walks to sofa down right and sits.* LOTTIE *follows quickly.)*

LOTTIE: Mr. Gregory will be the death of us! Just sitting in that room upstairs all day, talking to himself. And what about that black valise he carried in the first day?

HATTIE: It was his suitcase, dear.

LOTTIE: It was not a suitcase!

HATTIE *(Dryly):* Well, it was certainly too small to hide a body.

LOTTIE *(Reflecting):* That's true. *(Suddenly)* But if the body were all in parts—you know what I mean.

HATTIE: You've been reading those dreadful detective stories again. Mr. Gregory is a very quiet man who just doesn't like to socialize with us. He's not like that young Barry Morton.

LOTTIE: Barry may be all right, but he's entirely too attentive to Mary.

HATTIE: I'm glad she has someone young to spend time with. *(Abruptly)* This isn't getting us anywhere. I wish you'd leave Mr. Gregory alone.

LOTTIE: I don't trust him.

HATTIE: That's no reason to persecute him. Now, why were you calling the police? Murder, indeed!

LOTTIE *(Tearfully):* That's right. Make fun of me. *(Dabs at eyes with handkerchief)* Well, I have the proof this time. I know that Mr. Gregory has murdered someone, and I'm going to prove it! *(Walks left, calls)* Katie! Katie! Will you come here a minute, please? *(Returns to sofa)* Katie will tell you all about it. Then, maybe you'll believe me! (KATIE, *a timid, middle-aged woman, enters left.*)

KATIE: You called me, Miss Lottie?

LOTTIE: Yes, Katie. *(Smugly)* Will you please tell my sister exactly what you saw in Mr. Gregory's room?

KATIE *(Frightened):* Oh, Miss Lottie! You promised that you wouldn't mention it.

LOTTIE: It's all right. No one's going to harm you.

KATIE *(Slowly):* Miss Hattie, you told me never to clean Mr. Gregory's room while he was up there.

HATTIE: That's right.

KATIE: I thought he was out this morning, so up I went with my dust pan and mop.

HATTIE: And what happened?

KATIE: I walked right in. And then—and there—*(Her voice breaks. She collects herself and continues.)* He was sitting there, fearsome and terrible, like some monster, right on the edge of the bed. He glared at me and shouted at me to leave.

HATTIE: That's hardly any reason to brand the man a murderer.

KATIE *(Excitedly):* It wasn't that! When I went in, I saw something on the bed. He covered it ever so fast, but I could see—I could see—*(Covers face with apron and sobs)*

LOTTIE *(To HATTIE):* You frightened her.

HATTIE *(Impatiently):* What did you see, Katie?

KATIE: There was something—I'm sure it was a *body*—on the bed.

HATTIE: Nonsense!

KATIE: It isn't nonsense, Miss Hattie. Something was dangling from under the sheet. Something white and terrible! *(Loudly)* I know it was someone's arm!

HATTIE *(Getting alarmed):* An arm?

KATIE: Yes, yes, an arm! Oh, it was terrible! I slammed the door and ran down into the kitchen. I met Miss Lottie. She could see I was upset, and she made me tell. She made me tell!

HATTIE: A body. I can't believe it! It must be your imagination.

LOTTIE: You're a fool, Hattie. Katie knows what she saw.

HATTIE: But it must have been something else. Why would Mr. Gregory have a body in his room?

LOTTIE *(Significantly):* The black suitcase! Those are the facts, whether you believe them or not!

HATTIE: Fiddlesticks! There hasn't been a murder in Centerville in thirty-five years. *(Shakes her head)* No, I won't believe it!

LOTTIE: Then you refuse to do anything about it?

HATTIE: What can I do? *(Sarcastically)* Should I call Mr. Gregory and say, "I beg your pardon, but is there a corpse in your room?" Lottie, it's ridiculous!

LOTTIE *(Firmly):* The police will do something about it!

HATTIE: I won't let you call the police to tell them this fantastic story! They'd think you were—very odd! Thank goodness there's one level-headed person in this house! (LOTTIE *sits on sofa.*)

LOTTIE *(Upset):* Don't believe me, if you don't want to, but I'm frightened—terrified! (HATTIE *joins* LOTTIE *on sofa.*)

HATTIE *(Putting her arm over* LOTTIE'*s shoulders; comfortingly):* There, there, dear. Everything's going to be all right. *(Brightly)* I'll tell you what! (LOTTIE *looks up.*) Mr. Gregory is out now, but he should be back soon. I'll question him about—everything!

KATIE *(Fearfully):* Oh, no, Miss Hattie. Don't tell him what I saw. We'll all be murdered in our beds!

HATTIE: Nonsense, Katie. There must be a simple explanation. *(Slowly)* There has to be a reasonable explanation. *(Quickly)* Katie, get the tea things ready. Mary and Barry will be back shortly.

KATIE *(Tearfully):* Yes, ma'am. *(Exits left)*

LOTTIE *(Slowly):* I think Katie's right. If we confront Mr. Gregory, there's no telling what he'll do.

HATTIE *(Determined):* I won't hear another thing about it. It's the only way—and you'll feel terribly foolish after it's all been explained. (MARY *and* BARRY, *a young couple, enter center. They take off their coats and place them on a chair near the door.* HATTIE *and* LOTTIE *are unaware of their presence and* HATTIE *continues, angrily.*) All this murder nonsense is ridiculous!

MARY *(Quickly):* What's all this talk about murder, Aunt Hattie? *(Walks downstage)*

HATTIE: It's nothing at all, Mary. Your Aunt Lottie's letting her imagination carry her away. *(Turns to* BARRY*)* How are you today, Barry?

BARRY: I'm always fine when I'm with your beautiful niece. *(To* LOTTIE*)* And where is your imagination carrying you, Miss Barnes?

LOTTIE: Believe me, it's not my imagination. It's serious business—criminal.

HATTIE *(Sighing):* Lottie thinks that Mr. Gregory is—

LOTTIE: Hattie, you're treating me as if *I'd* committed some crime!

HATTIE: Well, you were going to call the police.

BARRY *(Uneasily):* The police? What for?

HATTIE: Nothing at all. Katie thought she saw a body in

Mr. Gregory's room, and Lottie is convinced that he's hiding a corpse! *(All laugh.* BARRY *watches* LOTTIE *steadily.)*

LOTTIE: Go ahead. Laugh if you wish. I know what I know, and facts are facts.

BARRY: But Mr. Gregory? Why, I've been living next to him for two weeks, and he seems just a harmless old codger.

LOTTIE *(Quickly):* I don't want to discuss this any more. *(Starts off)* I'm going to help Katie with the tea. *(Exits left)*

MARY: Poor Aunt Lottie!

BARRY: I hope we haven't hurt her feelings.

HATTIE *(Smugly):* She'll get over it.

BARRY: Tea sounds good to me. I'm hungry after chasing around town all day.

MARY *(Laughing):* Barry's a terrible shopper. *(To* BARRY) By the way, where did you go for that hour I was in the department store?

BARRY: I'll tell you later.

MARY *(Quickly):* Oh, Aunt Hattie, everybody in town is terribly upset about the robbery at the Updykes.

HATTIE: A robbery? Our paper hasn't come for two days, so I haven't read a thing about it.

MARY: Well, it seems that the Updykes held a benefit at their house for the local charities. It was quite an affair—music, a lavish buffet, entertainment, the works! After everyone left, Mrs. Updyke went to her room and found the wall safe opened.

BARRY: A diamond necklace and several diamond rings were missing. The thief didn't leave a trace. It was a professional job, all right!

MARY: One of the guests might have done it. After all, there were a hundred people in the house. Any one of them could have gone to Mrs. Updyke's bedroom unnoticed, and ransacked the safe. (LOTTIE *re-enters left, carrying tea tray with teapot, cups, saucers, etc.* BARRY *goes to her, takes tray and sets it on table center. He bends over tray, his back to audience.*)

HATTIE *(Pointing to table near sofa):* Oh, Barry, I think it would be better if you put the tray over here. (BARRY *moves tray.* HATTIE *starts to pour cups of tea.*)

LOTTIE: Katie is fixing some sandwiches. She'll bring them in in a moment.

MARY: Let's give Katie a hand, Barry.

BARRY: With pleasure. *(Arm in arm, they exit left.)*

LOTTIE: That Barry!

HATTIE *(Handing* LOTTIE *cup of tea): Now* what's the matter, Lottie?

LOTTIE *(Sighing):* I don't know. I just don't trust him.

HATTIE: He seems like a very nice young man, and Mary seems to find him attractive. *(Sips her tea)*

LOTTIE: In our day, a young woman was more careful about strangers.

HATTIE: Goodness! You're suspicious of everyone today!

LOTTIE: I don't trust him, no matter what you say.

HATTIE: You'll never trust our boarders. Barry's a nice young man, and Mary enjoys his company.

LOTTIE: Why doesn't she see that nice Rod Danvers any more?

HATTIE: Rod's a fine man, but a young detective doesn't have much free time. He's out at all hours on his cases and investigations.

LOTTIE: Rod is much more suitable for Mary, and I'm going to do something about it!

HATTIE *(Dryly):* I hope you're not planning to call the police again.

LOTTIE: Never mind! Two strangers in our house! Mr. Gregory and now this Barry Morton.

HATTIE *(Strongly):* You have to stop criticizing our boarders. You know we need the income. (LOTTIE *sips tea.*)

LOTTIE: This tea is bitter. What did Katie do to it? *(Replaces cup and saucer on tray)*

HATTIE: Mine tasted all right. *(Drains cup)* Lottie, you've been acting so strangely lately. Maybe you should see a doctor.

LOTTIE: Maybe so, but right now I'm going to learn the truth about Mr. Gregory before it's too late! *(Exits center, as* BARRY *and* MARY *enter left.* MARY *is frowning.)*

MARY: What happened to Aunt Lottie? She seemed so upset.

HATTIE: She's convinced that Mr. Gregory is an arch-criminal!

BARRY: I forgot something in my room. I'll be right back. *(Walks left, turns)* Mary, will you tell your aunt while I'm gone? *(Exits left)*

HATTIE: Tell me what, Mary?

MARY *(Slowly):* Barry's leaving here tomorrow.

HATTIE: Oh, I'm sorry to hear that.

MARY: His company called him back to the city. He didn't tell me until a few minutes ago, when we were in the kitchen. He went to the travel agency for his tickets while I was shopping.

HATTIE: I'm so sorry, Mary. I know you'll miss him.

MARY *(Dejectedly):* He said he may be back in a week or two, but who knows? (BARRY *re-enters.*)

HATTIE: We're going to miss you, Barry.

BARRY: Cheer up! I'll be back soon, and then wild horses won't be able to drag me away! (ROD DANVERS *enters center.*)

ROD: Hello, everybody!

HATTIE: Why, Rod Danvers! How nice!

ROD: The front door was open and I walked right in. I hope you don't mind. *(He glances uneasily at* MARY.)

HATTIE: We haven't seen you in ages.

ROD: I know. It's been busy at the office, and I'm taking my promotional exams right now.

MARY: Hello, Rod. I'm glad to see you again. *(Quickly)* I'd like you to meet one of our guests. *(She turns to* BARRY.)

Barry Morton—Rod Danvers. *(Greetings are exchanged.)*

ROD *(To* HATTIE): Actually, I'm here on business. Lieutenant Fletcher got a strange phone call a little while ago.

HATTIE: Oh, really?

ROD: Someone wanted to report a murder. The caller mentioned the name Hattie, and said that she lived on Maple Street. It was pretty easy to trace the call.

HATTIE *(Shaking head):* That Lottie!

ROD: Did your sister make the call?

HATTIE: Yes, she did. I tried to stop her, but without luck, obviously.

ROD: Maybe you'd like to tell me about it. Murder is serious business.

HATTIE: Really, it's all so silly. I think Lottie should tell you about it herself. I'll get her. She's upstairs. *(Exits)*

BARRY: Well, I have a little more packing to do. See you later. *(Exits)*

ROD: Why the cold shoulder, Mary? . . . *(Shrugs)* I guess I can't blame you, though. But you know how important my work is to me. I suppose I couldn't expect you to wait.

MARY *(Uncomfortably):* It isn't that. *(Rises)* Rod, I've lived in this house with Aunt Hattie and Aunt Lottie since I was a little girl. It hasn't been easy for them, or for me.

ROD: I know.

MARY: And Barry, the boarder you just met, is very attentive. It's been fun having someone young and lively around.

ROD *(Suddenly):* Is it serious?

MARY: Oh, no! I've known him only a couple of weeks, and he's leaving tomorrow.

ROD *(Nodding):* I know.

MARY: How could you know?

ROD: Remember, I'm a detective. I checked the travel agencies in town. Barry made reservations for the city this afternoon.

MARY *(Puzzled):* Why are you so interested in him?

ROD: We're interested in every stranger who was here when the Updyke jewels were stolen.

MARY: But he's never even been to the Updyke place.

ROD: Perhaps that's true, but we have to check everyone. The Updyke case is a tough one. The Updykes knew every guest in their house that night, except the entertainers and caterers, of course.

MARY: What kind of entertainers did they have?

ROD: Musicians, a fortuneteller, a ventriloquist—anything unusual to draw a crowd. The police are checking all the angles. *(Abruptly)* But let's forget about shop talk. I'm sorry I haven't been around much lately. I'd like to make up for lost time.

MARY: I don't know.

ROD: My exams will be over soon and—please, Mary—

MARY: Well, you can call if you like.

ROD *(Happily):* Great! I'm glad I'll be in the running again.

MARY *(Slowly):* Right now, I hope you'll be able to help us with Aunt Lottie.

ROD: What about this murder business?

MARY: I don't think it's anything. There's a certain boarder—a Mr. Gregory—that Aunt Lottie doesn't like. It's foolish, but she thinks he has a corpse in his room!

ROD *(Musing):* I guess I'm going to have more trouble with her than I thought.

MARY: Aunt Lottie's always been very fond of you, Rod. She'll listen to you.

ROD: I'll do my best.

MARY: It'll mean a lot to us. Aunt Hattie's very upset about the whole business.

ROD: I can imagine! *(Slowly)* Mysterious boarders—corpses in bedrooms—what next? (HATTIE, LOTTIE *and* BARRY *enter center.*)

LOTTIE *(Happily):* I knew the police would help me. I'm so glad they sent you, Rod.

ROD: Hi, Aunt Lottie! Mary tells me there have been some strange doings around here.

LOTTIE: Yes, indeed!

HATTIE *(Impatiently):* Rod, don't listen to her!

ROD: If you think there's any skullduggery afoot, we just have to ask Mr. Gregory about it. That shouldn't be too hard.

LOTTIE *(Quickly):* Then you know about him? *(To* HATTIE) You see? Mr. Gregory probably has a record a mile long. *(Extends her arms)*

ROD *(Shaking his head):* He doesn't have a record as far as I know. Mary told me about him.

LOTTIE *(Disappointed):* Oh! Well, I'm still sure that something is wrong. (MR. GREGORY *enters center, unseen by others. He looks and speaks like a Shakespearean actor.*)

ROD *(Sighing):* I'll question Gregory, if it will make you feel better.

LOTTIE *(Cautiously):* No. If you do that, you'll put him on guard. Why don't you search his room?

HATTIE: Mr. Gregory is out now, Rod. I don't know when he'll be back.

GREGORY *(Moving center):* I have returned, Miss Barnes. *(Bows with a flourish)*

HATTIE *(Aside, but audibly):* Oh, heavens! I hope you didn't hear us!

GREGORY: Unfortunately, I did. I've heard everything *(To* ROD) You are a member of the local police force, I presume. (ROD *nods.* GREGORY *walks to sofa, and sits.*) It's been a trying day, indeed! My profession is not an easy one.

LOTTIE *(Sarcastically):* I'm sure it isn't!

GREGORY *(Softly):* My dear Miss Barnes, why do you distrust me? I suppose it's because of the babbling of that foolish maid?

HATTIE: I'm sure you can explain everything.

GREGORY: I presume you would like to see my room.

ROD: I don't have a search warrant.

GREGORY *(Grandly)*: You may proceed without one.

LOTTIE *(Quickly)*: Ask him about the black bag, Rod.

ROD: Black bag?

LOTTIE: Yes, it's like a doctor's valise, but bigger.

GREGORY: I'll be happy to get that for the detective, too. (*To* BARRY) May I have the bag, young man?

BARRY *(Uncomfortably)*: Yes, sure. It's where you left it—in my room.

LOTTIE: What is your bag doing in Barry's room?

GREGORY: Everything will be answered in due time, Miss Barnes. (*To* ROD) Will you come along with me, please? *(Dramatically)* I don't want you to think I have destroyed the evidence. (ROD *and* GREGORY *exit.*)

HATTIE: Mr. Gregory is such a fine gentleman.

LOTTIE: Fiddlesticks! He's the criminal type, if I ever saw one. *(Waves finger at* BARRY) And what are *you* doing with his bag?

BARRY: Mr. Gregory will explain that.

LOTTIE *(Sarcastically)*: Oh, yes! I'm sure he'll have an answer for everything.

HATTIE: Goodness, this business has left me exhausted. (KATIE *enters left.*)

KATIE: The sandwiches are ready now. Shall I serve them?

HATTIE: Just put them on the table.

KATIE *(Cautiously)*: Are the police here?

HATTIE *(Sharply)*: Yes, thanks to *your* imagination. Katie, why didn't you tell *me* what you saw?

KATIE: I was frightened, so I told Miss Lottie.

HATTIE: Well, the damage is done. Mr. Morton is leaving tomorrow, and I'm sure Mr. Gregory won't spend another night in this house after all this fuss.

KATIE *(Tearfully)*: I'm sorry, Miss Barnes.

HATTIE: Don't start crying! I couldn't stand that now.

KATIE: I'd better get back to my kitchen. (KATIE *exits.*)

MARY: Poor Katie! She can cry easier than anyone I know. (ROD *and* GREGORY *return.* ROD *carries a black bag, which he places on center table.*)

ROD: This is the bag, Aunt Lottie. It was in Mr. Morton's room.

GREGORY: But I told you that. (LOTTIE *walks to table quickly and examines bag.*)

LOTTIE: Yes, I'm sure it's the same bag. Did you examine Mr. Gregory's room?

ROD *(Lightly):* I looked around. No corpses!

LOTTIE: Humph!

GREGORY: I'd like *you* to open the bag, Miss Lottie. I'm sure it will explain everything.

LOTTIE *(Anxiously):* Well, I don't know—

HATTIE: Open the bag, Lottie! You've gone this far! (*Slowly,* LOTTIE *unsnaps the two locks, lifts the top, and looks cautiously into bag.*)

LOTTIE: There's a cloth covering inside.

GREGORY *(Unconcerned):* Lift the covering, please! (LOTTIE *lifts cloth covering, reaches into bag, and takes out a dummy's head. She holds it up by its long blonde hair.* HATTIE *and* MARY *scream.* LOTTIE, *not quite realizing what she's holding, looks at it, and screaming, drops it onto table.*)

LOTTIE: A woman's head! I knew it! (*Everyone ad libs screams and exclamations.* ROD *picks up the head.*)

ROD: This is your corpse, Aunt Lottie—a dummy's head.

LOTTIE: A dummy? (*Reluctantly, she peers at head closely.*)

MARY: It looks so real! (*Runs her fingers across dummy's head*) Why, it feels like skin!

GREGORY: I tried to make it as realistic as possible. My work, you know.

LOTTIE: But Katie saw an arm!

GREGORY: To be sure! (*Amused*) We have quite an assortment. (*Takes out two dummy arms and legs from bag. One of the legs is broken.* ROD *points at bag.*)

ROD: Mr. Gregory is an entertainer. He's booked as the Great Gregory. Special shows, benefit performances.

LOTTIE *(Suspiciously):* Just what is your specialty, Mr. Gregory?

GREGORY *(Proudly):* I'm an accomplished ventriloquist. In the old days, I had steady bookings. Good houses, too! *(Sighs)* Now, show business has no room for ventriloquists, so Genevieve and I have to be content with whatever comes our way.

HATTIE: Genevieve? (GREGORY *laughs and points to the dummy.*)

GREGORY: I call my dummy Genevieve. We have worked together for a long, long time.

LOTTIE: But why didn't you explain all that to Katie? Why did you frighten her?

GREGORY: We professionals must have our little trade secrets. For years, my audience has accepted Genevieve as a real, live, precocious little girl. To see her unassembled—a few scattered pieces—would obviously ruin the illusion. *(To* BARRY*)* This young man was the only one in my confidence.

BARRY *(Nodding):* I mentioned that I was going to the city, so Mr. Gregory asked me to do an errand for him.

GREGORY *(Holding up broken leg parts):* I dropped Genevieve and broke one of her legs. A tragedy. I have to get it repaired, so I told Mr. Morton all about Genevieve, and he was kind enough to volunteer to take my Genevieve to the city and have the leg repaired. That's the whole story!

BARRY: I'm going to bring the dummy back in a week or two. Mr. Gregory asked me to keep his secret about the ventriloquist act. *(To* ROD*)* I hope there won't be any trouble about this.

ROD: It seems all right to me. *(To* GREGORY*)* I suppose you have no engagements for the next few weeks.

GREGORY: Alas, no! Fortune has chosen to frown upon me in recent years.

ROD: That wraps up our murder case!

HATTIE *(Embarrassed):* I don't know what to say. Mr. Gregory, will you ever forgive us?

GREGORY *(Grandly):* Of course! That incident is forgotten.

LOTTIE: I feel terribly foolish.

HATTIE *(Abruptly):* You should!

LOTTIE *(Suddenly):* And I don't feel very well.

HATTIE *(Relenting):* I'll take you to your room. You can rest before dinner. It's been a terrible day for us all. *(She and LOTTIE exit.)*

BARRY: I'll go along to my room. I still have some packing to do.

GREGORY *(Quickly):* You will not forget Genevieve, will you?

BARRY: I won't forget. I'll pick it up later. Don't worry. *(Exits)*

GREGORY: I must record this event for my memoirs. *(Stands)* It isn't often that I'm the prime suspect in a murder investigation. *(Exits. MARY smiles at ROD.)*

MARY *(Warmly, to ROD):* I hope we'll see you again soon, Rod.

ROD: Do you really mean that, Mary? *(She nods quickly. He takes his hat from chair, smiles broadly, and walks to exit.)* I'd better get back to the headquarters and report our "murder." But I'll call you, Mary—very soon. *(Exits center. Left alone, MARY lifts dummy's head, and starts to return it to bag. Suddenly she stops and shakes head. She examines head closely, presses her fingers against the back. The material gives way and a diamond bracelet and several diamond rings fall out.)*

MARY *(Picking up jewels):* Diamonds! The Updyke diamonds! Of course! The benefit performance. *(Excitedly)* Rod said there was a ventriloquist's act at the party! Mr.

Gregory! That's why he came here. *(Panicky)* I have to call Rod right away. *(Quickly she picks up dummy's head and stuffs it into bag with jewels, and slams bag closed, as* BARRY *enters center. She is unaware of his presence. She quickly picks up the phone, and* BARRY *crosses the stage. He puts his hand over the phone.* MARY *turns with frightened scream.)* Oh, Barry! You frightened me! Thank heavens it's you.

BARRY *(Coolly):* What's the matter, Mary?

MARY *(Excitedly):* Aunt Lottie was right about Mr. Gregory! He stole the Updyke jewels after all, and hid them in the dummy's head.

BARRY: What are you talking about? (MARY *points to bag.*)

MARY: I found the jewels—there in that bag! A diamond bracelet, diamond rings—everything! *(Quickly)* Don't you see? He was at the Updyke house that night doing his ventriloquist's act. He stole the jewels and hid them in the dummy's head.

BARRY: Now, take it easy. Someone else might have put them in the dummy. We can't accuse Gregory again, without being sure of our facts.

MARY: I'm going to call Rod right away. He'll know what to do.

BARRY *(Firmly):* I wouldn't advise you to call the police.

MARY: Why not? Someone has to call them. *(Trailing off, suddenly)* Wait a minute! The dummy was in your room!

BARRY: Mary!

MARY *(Drawing away from him):* And you were planning to leave tomorrow. That's it! You're Gregory's accomplice. You were going to take the dummy away under the pretext of having the leg mended. Of course! You planned to sell the jewels in the city, or maybe out of the country.

BARRY *(Heatedly):* You don't know what you're talking about.

MARY *(Quickly):* Gregory was afraid that the police might be suspicious of him, knowing that he was at the Updyke house, so he used you to dispose of the jewels. That's why you came here at the same time as Gregory. It was part of a carefully worked out plan! (BARRY *steps closer, grabs her arm.*)

BARRY *(Coldly):* You're pretty clever. Too clever, I think.

MARY *(Anxiously):* You won't get away with it, Barry. The police know that you're leaving town tomorrow. Rod told me that you're under investigation.

BARRY *(Nodding):* The police in this hick town are smarter than I thought. I'm afraid my original plans have to be altered. Gregory and I will have to leave together. But we can't wait until tomorrow. We'll have to leave now— tonight! (MARY *glances toward exit.*) Don't try to call your aunts. They won't hear you.

MARY: What have you done to them?

BARRY: Tea is most restful for the nerves. And, of course, I helped things along with a sedative.

MARY: The tea! You put something in the tea!

BARRY *(Nodding):* I couldn't have those meddlesome old women interfere. They'll sleep very peacefully until tomorrow morning.

MARY: And Katie—

BARRY *(Smiling):* I'm sure Katie is enjoying her beauty nap in the kitchen right now. She had some tea, too! *(Ominously)* There's only one person standing in my way right now, Mary. That's you! It's unfortunate that you found the jewelry. I was beginning to like you.

MARY *(Fearfully):* What are you going to do?

BARRY: I'm going to keep you from calling the police. *(Grabs phone and rips cord out of wall)* There! *(Holds up end of cord)* I don't think you'll use that tonight. This will come in very handy to see that you stay put. (MARY *attempts to struggle but* BARRY *throws cord over her shoulder, attempting to encircle her throat.* GREGORY *appears in center entrance, looking depressed.*) Don't just stand there, Gregory. Help me tie her up. We have to get out of here. She found the jewels!

GREGORY *(Feebly):* I'm sorry, m'lad. The best laid schemes and all that! *(He slowly walks center, followed by* ROD *and* LIEUTENANT FLETCHER. *They carry drawn revolvers.)* We have two callers, you see.

BARRY *(Dropping cord):* The police!

FLETCHER *(To* ROD): Your hunch was right, Rod. I'll get these two down to headquarters. The squad car is outside. (MARY *drops down onto sofa.)* You might give this young woman *(Points to* MARY) some attention.

ROD *(Crossing to* MARY): Are you all right, Mary? *(She nods mutely.)* I hope this guy didn't give you a hard time. *(Points revolver at* BARRY) I knew he was planning to leave town, and the Lieutenant learned something else, too. Barry made another reservation in the city—a reservation on a plane to Amsterdam!

FLETCHER: Right. The diamond capital of the world! It didn't take much after that to tell us we were on the right trail. *(Motioning to* BARRY *and* GREGORY *with gun)* All right, you guys, you have a date at headquarters!

MARY: The diamonds are in the black bag. (FLETCHER *takes the bag with his free hand.)*

FLETCHER: I guess this is the bag you told me about, Rod. (ROD *nods.)* Well, maybe the ventriloquist's dummy will start talking at headquarters, too! *(He pushes* BARRY *and* GREGORY *ahead of him to center exit.* GREGORY *turns.)*

GREGORY *(Dramatically):* All the world's a stage!

FLETCHER: O.K., Macbeth, get going! *(They exit.)*

ROD: Fletcher's not up on his Shakespeare, but he's a first-rate detective. (MARY *rises suddenly.)*

MARY: I almost forgot. Aunt Hattie! Aunt Lottie! Barry drugged their tea. I must get them at once. (LOTTIE *and* HATTIE *enter center,* LOTTIE *supporting* HATTIE *by the arm.)*

LOTTIE: That won't be necessary, Mary. I can take care of myself.

MARY: Aunt Lottie! Thank goodness you're all right!

LOTTIE: Of course, I'm all right, but Hattie needs a bit of

attention. *(Proudly)* For the first time in my life, *I've* been able to look after *her.*

MARY: But how—why didn't *you* drink the tea?

LOTTIE: Fiddlesticks! There's one thing you can never fool me with—and that's my tea! I knew there was something wrong with it when I took the first sip.

MARY: Why did you pretend to be sleepy?

LOTTIE: No one would have believed me then if I said the tea was doctored. I had to let Mr. Gregory play out his hand. *(Smugly)* Yes, sir! I've learned a lot in those true detective books!

ROD *(Laughing):* If there are any vacancies down at headquarters, I'll keep you in mind. *(Leads HATTIE to sofa)* Are you all right, Aunt Hattie?

HATTIE *(Slowly):* Yes, I—I think so, but *(Putting her hand on her head)* my poor head! I don't know what I would have done if Lottie hadn't kept putting those cold cloths on my head to keep me awake.

MARY: What about Katie? We'd better see how she is.

LOTTIE: Heavens, yes! Poor thing. *(To HATTIE)* If we're going to take any more boarders, I'm going to approve of them—first!

HATTIE *(Meekly):* Anything you say, Lottie.

ROD: I don't know about boarders, but I have a hunch you'll be losing a tenant very shortly.

LOTTIE: What do you mean, Rod?

ROD *(Grinning):* I'm going to ask your niece to change her address! *(He smiles warmly at MARY, who returns his smile. They walk toward each other as curtain falls.)*

THE END

Production Notes

I Want to Report a Murder

Characters: 4 male; 4 female.

Playing Time: 30 minutes.

Costumes: Katie wears black dress, white apron, and carries hand-kerchief. Mary, Barry, Fletcher and Rod wear coats upon their first appearance. Mr. Gregory is dressed in a dark suit. He wears a shoestring tie and carries a wide-brimmed hat. His clothes are typical of an old Shakespearean actor.

Properties: Handkerchief, tea tray with teapot, cups and saucers; black valise containing dummy with unassembled head, legs, arms and torso (a large doll may be used); diamond bracelet and rings; revolvers.

Setting: An old-fashioned living room. Entrance is upstage center. If desired, a staircase may be seen through the entrance. Another entrance, at left, leads to the dining room and kitchen. A sofa and table are downstage right. Another table with a telephone on it is beside a chair downstage left. There is a large round table downstage center. The furniture is old-fashioned.

Lighting: No special effects.

Airport Adventure

Characters

SERGEANT MURPHY, *security guard*
JIM DAWSON, *scientist*
SANDRA BENNETT, *his assistant*
DAVE HARRISON
MRS. WAVERLY KIRKWOOD III
ALICE PALMER
MR. PORTER
PROFESSOR STAPLETON
JANE DUMONT, *ticket agent*
PASSENGERS ⎫
AIRLINE PERSONNEL ⎪ *extras*
INFORMATION CLERKS ⎬
OFFSTAGE VOICE ⎭

SETTING: *International Airport terminal. Ticket counter is up center. There are arrival and departure schedules behind it. Up left is information desk, with sign. Several telephones are on counter down right, with large city phone books near them. Chairs, benches, plants complete the setting. The atmosphere conveyed should be one of constant activity, with passengers and airline personnel hurrying through the terminal, throughout the play.*

AT RISE: PASSENGERS *and* AIRLINE PERSONNEL *(pilots, flight attendants, baggage personnel, etc.) enter and exit throughout play.* JANE DUMONT *stands behind ticket counter.* INFORMATION CLERKS *talk with* PASSENGERS *at desk.* SERGEANT MUR-

PHY *stands down left.* OFFSTAGE VOICE *is heard intermittently, announcing flights.* JIM DAWSON *and* SANDRA BENNETT *enter, followed by* DAVE HARRISON. JIM *carries a coat over his right arm, concealing his briefcase.* SANDRA *is pinning a corsage to her suit.*

DAVE *(Singing to tune of "Here Comes the Bride"):* Dum-dum-da-dum! *(Speaking)* Behold the happily married couple!

JIM: For Pete's sake, Dave, cool it.

DAVE *(Loudly):* Shout it to the world. Behold the newlyweds! *(Passersby smile and nod knowingly.* SERGEANT MURPHY *strides forward.* DAVE *reaches into his pocket, then throws handful of rice at* JIM *and* SANDRA, *but* JIM *ducks and rice hits* MURPHY *in face.)*

JIM: I—I'm sorry, Officer.

MURPHY: Sergeant Murphy, to you!

JIM: Sergeant Murphy, I *am* sorry. My friend, here, just got carried away.

DAVE: They're off on their honeymoon, Sergeant.

MURPHY *(Mellowing):* A honeymoon, is it?

JIM *(Awkwardly):* I'm Jim Dawson, and this is my bride, Sandra Bennett—er—Sandra *Dawson.*

MURPHY *(To* JIM): I hope you two will be very happy. *(He brushes rice from his hair, goes left and resumes post.)*

JIM: Thanks, Sergeant. *(Pauses, then to* DAVE) Any more of that, Dave, and I'll spend my honeymoon in jail. *(Quietly)* How am I doing?

DAVE *(In low tone):* Pretty good, Jim. I'm trying to put it over, this honeymoon bit. But watch the "Sandra Bennett" stuff. She's Sandra Dawson now. *(In loud voice)* I suppose the newlyweds want to be alone.

SANDRA: Our connecting flight for Switzerland will be leaving soon. You've been wonderful, Dave. Such a lovely corsage. It was so thoughtful of you to buy it for me.

DAVE: My pleasure, Sandra. *(Takes a ticket envelope from his pocket and hands it to* JIM, *who takes it with his left hand)* Your tickets, Jim. One week in Switzerland—you lucky newlyweds! *(Quietly)* Good luck, Jim. Remember, everything depends on this trip.

SANDRA: Goodbye, Dave. You've been a wonderful best man. *(He pats her arm affectionately.)*

DAVE *(In low tone):* Take care, Sandra, and help Jim. *(In a loud voice)* And keep your husband away from the Swiss misses. *(He waves, exits right.)*

SANDRA *(Nervously):* I'm frightened, Jim.

JIM: Don't worry. Nothing can go wrong. *(He lifts coat on his right arm, revealing the briefcase handcuffed to his wrist.)* These top-secret plans for the nuclear bomb site will be in the hands of our agent in Switzerland tomorrow, right on schedule.

SANDRA: But what if the plans should fall into the wrong hands?

JIM: Not a chance. When Professor Stapleton chose us to be the couriers, he set up this fake honeymoon so no one would suspect the real purpose of the trip. He's taken care of every detail.

SANDRA: But I'm afraid we're being followed. There was a suspicious-looking man near the flower stand outside when Dave bought the corsage. He may be here now, watching us—waiting to steal the plans.

JIM: Well, if he takes the plans, he'll have to take me, too. It was a good idea of Stapleton's—shackling the briefcase to my wrist. *(Holds up arm, revealing handcuffs)*

SANDRA: Please, Jim—someone might see. *(He lowers arm.)*

JIM: You know, this is the most exciting thing that's happened to me since I joined Dr. Stapleton's nuclear physics department. Here I am on an important mission, with an attractive wife—and it's all happened within twenty-four hours!

SANDRA: I know you're doing everything to keep up my courage, Jim, but I'm still afraid. *(Suddenly)* He's there! He's right out there watching us. The same man! (JIM *turns quickly.)*

JIM: Who? Where?

SANDRA: Oh, he's gone now. But he must have seen us. It's the same man, Jim.

JIM: Your imagination is playing tricks on you.

SANDRA *(Insistently):* No. It was the same man. He's wearing a dark hat and coat.

JIM: It was probably just another passenger.

SANDRA *(Nervously):* If the plans ever fell into enemy hands—*(She shivers and touches her forehead.)* All this excitement is too much for me. My head feels so strange.

JIM: Maybe it's all that rich food you ate in the restaurant Dave took us to. *(He gives tickets to* SANDRA.) Keep the tickets in your purse, will you? *(She puts tickets into purse.)*

SANDRA: Sure. I'm going to get some water and take a couple of aspirins. Maybe they'll help.

JIM: Good idea. *(Points to seats up right)* I'll wait over there. (SANDRA *exits left, and* JIM *sits on bench, carefully covering the briefcase with his coat. After a few moments,* ALICE PALMER *enters left. She resembles* SANDRA, *and wears a suit and corsage nearly identical to* SANDRA's. *Seeing her,* JIM *stands and goes to meet her. She smiles.)* That was quick! How's your headache? *(He stares closely at her.)* Oh, I'm sorry. I—I mistook you for someone else. *(Starts to turn away)*

ALICE: Darling, was I terribly long? My makeup was such a fright—you must forgive me. (JIM *stares at her with amazement.)*

JIM: Who are you? You're not Sandra!

ALICE *(Innocently):* What's the matter with you, Jim? (JIM *pushes her aside, looks at left exit.* MURPHY *watches him with interest.)*

JIM *(Attempting to control his voice):* What have you done to Sandra?

ALICE: I don't know what you're talking about. Really, darling, you're frightening me.

JIM: Look, I'm wise to your game. And if you've done anything to Sandra . . .

ALICE *(Soothingly):* Jim, keep your voice down. People are watching us. *(She pretends embarrassment as she glances around and smiles awkwardly at passersby.)*

JIM: I'll take this place apart, brick by brick, until I find Sandra! (MURPHY *walks forward.*)

MURPHY: Is something wrong?

ALICE: Of course not. My husband is a little disturbed because we've had such a hectic day!

JIM: There's plenty wrong, Sergeant Murphy. Something's happened to my wife.

MURPHY: She looks all right to me.

JIM: But this is not my wife. Sandra's disappeared. (ALICE *looks at* MURPHY *and shrugs.*)

ALICE: You must recognize me, Sergeant Murphy.

MURPHY *(Scratching his head):* Well, you look like his wife. She was wearing the same flowers a little while ago.

JIM *(Desperately):* Sergeant, you're just remembering the flowers. This is not the same person. This woman's *not* my wife.

MURPHY: That must have been some wedding reception, young fellow.

JIM *(Insistently):* I know what I'm talking about. You must believe me.

MURPHY *(To* ALICE): Does he get like this often?

ALICE: It's the first time. I don't know what to do.

MURPHY: Well, I think he needs a good rest. When does your flight leave?

JIM *(Suddenly):* The flight! Yes, that's it! Sandra would know all about the flight. Sergeant, ask *her* about the flight. What time? What flight number?

ALICE *(Patiently):* But we went over that so many times. Really, Jim! We're taking flight 321 for Geneva by way of London. It leaves tonight at ten o'clock.

MURPHY: There *is* a trans-atlantic flight that leaves then.

JIM: She must have found out about our reservations. She works for . . . well, never mind, but she's up to no good.

ALICE *(Annoyed):* Jim Dawson! If you persist with this nonsense, I'll insist that we leave for home immediately.

MURPHY: Perhaps that would be best.

JIM: I'm not leaving here until I find Sandra. *(Suddenly)* The tickets! I gave Sandra our tickets. *(To* ALICE) Where are they now?

ALICE: Why, I have them right here, Jim, in my purse. *(She takes out tickets and hands them to* MURPHY, *who examines them and returns them to her.)* Two tickets to Geneva, Switzerland.

MURPHY: That's right.

JIM: Then she has done something to Sandra. Sandra had those tickets in her purse when she went to take some aspirin. *(To* ALICE) You took them from her. Sergeant, she told me a man in a dark hat and coat followed us to the airport. That man and this woman did something to Sandra. (MURPHY *and* ALICE *look at each other and shrug.)* Sergeant, you must believe me. This woman is an impostor. She's not the one I'm supposed to have married.

MURPHY: *Supposed* to have married?

JIM: Yes, Sandra, the woman I came in with. I'm not married to her, either.

MURPHY *(To* ALICE): I think this fellow is balmy. *(Points to* JIM's *coat)* I've watched the way you've been holding that coat. What are you hiding? *(He pulls coat aside.)* Handcuffs? What is this?

JIM: Top security. My boss, Professor Stapleton, has the only key to these handcuffs in this country.

ALICE *(Impatiently):* Those handcuffs were snapped on my husband's wrist as a prank at the wedding reception. We were going to have them removed by a locksmith. Jim, maybe we can find a locksmith now, before we board.

MURPHY: Not so fast, young lady. I'd like to have a look at that briefcase.

JIM *(Hoarsely):* No! No! No one is allowed to see the contents of this briefcase, except Dr. Stapleton and his colleague in Geneva.

MURPHY: This gets crazier by the minute.

ALICE *(Firmly):* Jim, I'm going to get us on board the plane right now so you can have a good rest.

JIM: Not on your life. I'm going to find Sandra Bennett. *(Suddenly)* I know! I'll call Professor Stapleton! Oh, why didn't I think of him before? I have his emergency number. He'll come to the airport and tell you this woman is an impostor.

MURPHY: I don't know what this is all about, but I'll call your Professor Stapleton from my office. You're coming with me. (MR. PORTER, *a tall man wearing a dark coat and hat and carrying a newspaper, enters.* ALICE *sees him, shakes her head, and turns to* MURPHY.)

ALICE: But this is completely ridiculous, Sergeant. I don't know any Professor Stapleton, and I don't want to miss our flight.

MURPHY: This won't take long, ma'am. Now, come along. *(They exit. As* ALICE *leaves, she signals* PORTER, *who sits on bench and reads paper.* MRS. WAVERLY KIRKWOOD III, *an imposing dowager, enters and goes to ticket counter.)*

JANE: Good evening. May I help you?

MRS. KIRKWOOD: I certainly hope so. I am Mrs. Waverly Kirkwood III, and it is imperative that I book passage on your very next flight to Phoenix, Arizona. My health, you know.

JANE: I'm terribly sorry, but our next Arizona flight is completely booked.

MRS. KIRKWOOD: Ridiculous! Have you no concern for my condition? My doctor insists there's nothing wrong with me. At fifty dollars a visit, you'd think he'd find a little something.

JANE *(Patiently):* There is another flight to Phoenix in three hours.

MRS. KIRKWOOD: Three hours? Impossible! My health will not permit it. I insist that you find a seat for me on the next flight, or it will be necessary for me to call the airline president. Personal friend of my dear, departed husband, you know. (JANE *sighs, picks up phone and pantomimes talking into it, while* MRS. KIRKWOOD *taps her fingers impatiently.* JANE *smiles, puts receiver down.*)

JANE: In view of the—ah—emergency, I think I can arrange passage on the next Arizona flight. (MRS. KIRKWOOD *nods triumphantly.*) It's a first-class, deluxe flight. We'll serve a dinner of *filet mignon,* broccoli hollandaise, and baked Alaska. There's also a first-run showing of the movie "Love Is the Thing."

MRS. KIRKWOOD *(Glumly):* Oh, dear. Perhaps I'd better wait for the flight in three hours.

JANE: But this is a first-class seat.

MRS. KIRKWOOD: Granted.

JANE: And excellent cuisine.

MRS. KIRKWOOD: But of course.

JANE *(Puzzled):* I don't understand. You were so anxious to get to Arizona.

MRS. KIRKWOOD: Oh, the flight is all right, and I know I'll enjoy the dinner. But that dreadful picture, "Love Is the Thing." I've already seen it. No, the flight won't do at all.

JANE *(Grimly):* I'll make a reservation for you on the following flight.

MRS. KIRKWOOD: Thank you, my dear. I'll take the next flight—but find out what's playing! (*She exits left.* JANE *shakes her head.* JIM, MURPHY, *and* ALICE *return left.* JIM *waves his arms frantically.*)

JIM: I can't help it if Professor Stapleton isn't at his apartment.

MURPHY: I should run you both in.

ALICE *(Determinedly):* I know my rights, Sergeant Murphy, and you're going to do nothing of the kind. My husband and I haven't committed any crime, and we're going to leave on our flight, as scheduled. I'll see that he gets a complete rest when we arrive in Switzerland.

MURPHY: Don't get highfalutin' with me, young lady.

ALICE: But we've done nothing wrong! My husband is just emotionally upset.

JIM: I am not emotionally upset! I just want to find Sandra Bennett!

MURPHY *(Firmly):* I'm going to call the lieutenant. He'll know what to do. You'd both better stay here.

ALICE: I won't let him out of my sight, Sergeant. (PORTER *discards his newspaper and stands.* MURPHY *exits left.)*

JIM: You're pretty clever, aren't you? Now, if you don't tell me what happened to Sandra, I'll—

ALICE: You're really in no position to make threats. *(She gestures in* PORTER'S *direction.)*

JIM *(Seeing* PORTER): The man in the dark coat and hat! Sandra was right. We were being followed.

ALICE: An amazing deduction! Now, my friend and I would like you to accompany us to a car waiting outside.

JIM: How are you planning to get me out of the terminal, with all these people around?

ALICE: It won't be difficult. *(She opens her purse and places her hand inside.)* I have a very effective weapon, you see.

JIM: A gun?

ALICE: And it's pointed directly at you, Mr. Dawson. Are you ready to come along? (PORTER *joins them, glances around cautiously.)* I'd like to introduce you to an old friend of mine—Mr. Porter. He's waiting to escort us out of here.

PORTER: A pleasure.

JIM *(Suddenly):* I'm not going!

PORTER: You're a fool.

ALICE: Let me handle this, Porter. Mr. Dawson, I'm going to count to three, and if you're not ready to leave, I'll shoot. One—two—

JIM: Will you promise not to harm Sandra?

ALICE: Ms. Bennett is perfectly safe, I assure you.

JIM *(Sighing):* O.K. I'll go.

PORTER: A very wise decision. It's quite important that we have that briefcase. (MURPHY *enters right, joins group, surprising* PORTER *and* ALICE. JIM *smiles with relief.*)

ALICE: Why, Sergeant Murphy, what a stroke of luck! I just met an old friend of ours. He doesn't think that Jim should travel tonight, so we're going to spend the evening in his apartment.

MURPHY *(Grimly):* You may all be spending the night behind bars. The lieutenant is coming down from headquarters. We're all going to wait right here, nice and quiet. He's bringing a set of master keys, too, just in case the groom hasn't taken leave of his senses.

JIM: No, no! You must not open the briefcase! It's vital to the security of the country.

MURPHY: Don't play cloak-and-dagger with me, young fellow!

PORTER: This is outrageous, Sergeant. You can't intimidate us.

MURPHY: Cut the fancy language! You're going to wait right here till the lieutenant comes.

JIM *(Happily):* That's the stuff, Sergeant! And, if you don't believe me, you can look in her purse. She—she has a gun. She threatened to kill me.

MURPHY *(Cautiously):* I'll take that purse, miss. *(Holds out his hand for it)*

ALICE: I've never been so humiliated.

MURPHY: The purse, if you please. *(She gives him the purse.* MURPHY *examines its contents thoroughly.)*

JIM *(Anxiously):* The gun! Did you find the gun?

MURPHY *(Sternly):* No, I didn't. The only weapons in here are a change purse, cosmetic kit, letters, tickets and a handkerchief. What made you think she had a gun?

JIM *(Desperately):* She said so. She threatened to kill me.

PORTER: It's obvious, Sergeant, that my friend is suffering

from mental strain. I can't permit you to jeopardize his health. He needs rest.

MURPHY *(Scratching his head):* Well, I don't know. This gun business really has me puzzled.

PORTER *(Threateningly):* I'll handle him, Sergeant.

JIM: Don't listen to them! They want to kill me and take the briefcase! *(A commotion is heard off left.* MRS. KIRKWOOD *enters, supporting a dazed* SANDRA, *who still wears her corsage.* ALICE *and* PORTER *exchange quick glances.* MURPHY *looks at* SANDRA, *then wheels on* ALICE *and* PORTER, *drawing his gun.* PORTER *turns to run, but* JIM *sticks out his foot and trips him.* MURPHY *grabs* ALICE'S *arm.* SANDRA *shakes her head dizzily, rushes to* JIM.)

SANDRA *(Weakly):* Oh, Jim!

JIM *(Hugging her):* Sandra, I'm so glad to see you! (MRS. KIRKWOOD *joins them, puts her arm around* SANDRA'S *shoulders.)*

MRS. KIRKWOOD: I found this poor thing lying on the sofa in the ladies' lounge. Countless people must have passed her and didn't raise a finger to help, but I knew she needed aid. I think she's been drugged!

SANDRA *(Pointing at* ALICE): That woman! I saw her in the lounge. I noticed her because she was wearing an outfit so similar to mine. *(She pauses, shakes her head.)* As we were talking, I blacked out. I don't know what happened after that.

JIM: Well, the important thing now is that you're O.K.

MURPHY *(Approaching them):* Is this the girl you married— er—you were supposed to marry?

JIM: Yes, Sergeant. She'll tell you my story is true. (PORTER *stands.* MURPHY *levels his gun.)*

MURPHY *(Pointing to* ALICE): And fake bride number two will have a lot of explaining to do. *(To* ALICE *and* PORTER) Come on, you two. The lieutenant is waiting for you. *(To* JIM) And both of you can come along in a little while. *(Points to* SANDRA) You'd better get that girl some water.

(MRS. KIRKWOOD *watches the proceedings with amazement.* PROFESSOR STAPLETON, *a scholarly, middle-aged man, rushes in, right.*)

STAPLETON: Sandra! Jim! Thank heavens you're safe!

SANDRA: Oh, Professor Stapleton!

STAPLETON: I entered my apartment just as the emergency phone stopped ringing. I knew that something must have gone wrong at the airport, so I rushed over here.

JIM: And not a minute too soon. The briefcase is safe, thank goodness—or rather, thanks to Sergeant Murphy. (*Points to* ALICE) That woman even threatened to shoot me.

SANDRA (*In dismay*): She was going to kill you?

JIM: No, she actually was bluffing. She didn't have a gun. It was a trick to get me to leave the airport. (*Grimly*) Sergeant Murphy, here, thought I was crazy. Oh, I don't know where to start. I'll tell you all about it later.

STAPLETON (*Staring at* ALICE): Why, I know this woman! Alice Palmer! She's wanted for questioning in a stolen missile-plans case.

ALICE (*Coolly*): Yes, Professor Stapleton. We meet again.

MURPHY: But not for long, young lady. I think the authorities will see to that. (*To* STAPLETON) Will you vouch for the identity of these young people? (*He gestures at* SANDRA *and* JIM.)

STAPLETON: Yes, of course. (JIM *grabs* ALICE's *arm.*)

JIM: I'd like the tickets, please. (ALICE *takes tickets from purse, hands them to* JIM.) I don't intend to go on a honeymoon—or anywhere else—with you tonight! (*He puts tickets in his left-hand pocket.* MURPHY, ALICE, PORTER *and* STAPLETON *exit left.* SANDRA *smiles weakly at* MRS. KIRKWOOD.)

SANDRA: How can I ever thank you?

MRS. KIRKWOOD: My child, I haven't had so much excitement in years. Those dreadful people! Drugging you!

SANDRA (*Slowly*): Yes, the drug—but I don't see how she

could have done it. She didn't offer me anything to eat. *(Shakes head.* JANE *calls from ticket counter.)*

JANE: Oh, Mrs. Kirkwood.

MRS. KIRKWOOD *(Turning):* Yes, my dear?

JANE: I made your reservation to Phoenix.

MRS. KIRKWOOD: Phoenix? Why, I have no intention of traveling at all, and I don't care about the old motion picture, either. There are far more exciting things right here in the airport terminal! *(Happily)* I've never felt better in my life. *(She exits.)*

JIM *(Solicitously):* Sandra, you'd better get back to your apartment.

SANDRA: My apartment? Don't be silly! I'm leaving for Switzerland with you.

JIM: But, Sandra, the enemy agents know all about the phony honeymoon now.

SANDRA: I don't care. I'm determined to make our mission successful in spite of it. Do you think I'd give up now? *(Angrily)* I've been drugged, threatened, and almost murdered, all in one evening! Now I'm angry. Nothing is going to interfere with our plans!

JIM: Good for you! You came through it all beautifully. Even your corsage—it's still fresh. *(Soberly)* But I'm still worried.

SANDRA: What about?

JIM: How did Porter and Alice Palmer know all about our plans? This honeymoon was arranged to conceal the true purpose of our flight. And yet they knew about our reservations—they knew about everything. And how were you drugged? You said that Alice didn't offer you anything to eat or drink.

SANDRA: Well, no, but—

JIM: Alice was waiting for the moment to assume your identity. Porter was right on the spot at the right moment. They knew everything about us—right down to the smallest detail.

SANDRA: Do you mean that someone else is involved?

JIM: Yes. Someone who must be very close to our activities. Someone who knew about our plans. Someone who informed Alice and Porter that we must be stopped at all costs.

SANDRA *(In disbelief)*: One of us?

JIM: That has to be the answer. *(Suddenly)* Why did Stapleton arrive on the scene so suddenly?

SANDRA: He told you that he heard his private phone ringing.

JIM: Yes. A convenient explanation. Too convenient, perhaps. . . . He might have been here all the time, watching us. Then, if anything went wrong with Porter and Alice's plans, he was ready to take over. I'd better get to Murphy's office—and fast!

SANDRA: I'm going with you.

JIM: No, you've had enough excitement for one night. There's not a minute to lose.

SANDRA: Jim—

JIM: Stay here. I'll be back soon. *(Starts left)*

SANDRA *(Calling after him)*: Oh, Jim—I—*(He exits left. SANDRA stares around, bewildered, looking at several passersby with suspicion. Nervously, she moves down left so she can watch both entrances to the airport. DAVE enters right, panting as if he has been running. SANDRA waves, runs to join him downstage.)* Oh, Dave, I'm so glad to see you. Something terrible has happened.

DAVE: What's the matter? Where's Jim?

SANDRA *(Gesturing)*: He's with the police. We caught two enemy agents who tried to steal the briefcase.

DAVE *(Anxiously)*: Where are the plans now?

SANDRA: The plans are safe. Jim still has them locked in the briefcase. Professor Stapleton is here, too. And Jim thinks . . .

DAVE *(Coldly)*: What does Jim think?

SANDRA: Oh, I'm so confused. I was drugged, you see, and everything is still hazy.

DAVE: Drugged?

SANDRA: One of the agents—Alice Palmer—must have done something to me. *(Stops)* But she had to know that I'd be at the airport. She was all ready to impersonate me, but *(Puzzled)* she didn't have a chance to drug me. That couldn't have been prearranged.

DAVE: What are you talking about?

SANDRA: I must have been drugged earlier in the evening. Maybe it was someone at that restaurant where you, Jim and I had dinner. *(Suddenly)* Jim is right! There is a spy in our team of nuclear physicists—someone who masterminded the whole thing!

DAVE: Don't be ridiculous.

SANDRA: Wait! Jim felt that someone close to us was responsible for the whole thing. Jim thought it was Stapleton. Someone who knew about our plans—someone who could have drugged my food—someone who could be with us without creating suspicion. *(She touches corsage.)* This flower! That's it!

DAVE: What about that flower? I gave it to you myself.

SANDRA *(Slowly)*: I know that, Dave. Alice Palmer couldn't possibly have known in advance what kind of corsage I would be wearing—unless someone told her. Yet she had an identical corsage. Someone must have given her the same corsage that I would be wearing. It had to be you, Dave.

DAVE: Sandra!

SANDRA *(Coldly)*: It had to be that way. You were at the restaurant. You could have drugged my food. When the drug had taken effect, Alice Palmer was prepared to assume my identity. Fortunately for her, everything went according to plan. I fainted in the ladies' room. If it hadn't happened then, it might have happened in the waiting room—or on the plane. Yes, Alice Palmer was even ready to make the flight in my place.

DAVE: I won't listen to this nonsense.

SANDRA *(Ignoring him):* And you left nothing to chance. You bought me this corsage, and you bought one for Alice, too, so she could impersonate me—right down to the same flower. You always were a perfectionist, Dave.

DAVE *(Nervously):* If I wanted the plans, why couldn't I have stolen them from the lab?

SANDRA: That way, you would have given your little show away. You wanted your henchmen to steal them so that you could continue to work with Dr. Stapleton—and block all our work for the future.

DAVE *(Menacingly):* A pretty little theory, but I doubt that you'll live to tell anyone about it. (SANDRA *quickly reaches inside her purse.*)

SANDRA: You can't win, Dave. I have a gun trained on you, a gun professor Stapleton gave me, and I'm not afraid to use it.

DAVE: Now, listen, Sandra—

SANDRA: No, it's your turn to listen—and to talk. *(She raises her purse.)*

DAVE: All right! Don't shoot. You're right—I arranged it all! Sandra, please—(MURPHY *and* JIM *enter left.* JIM *rushes to* DAVE *and grapples with him with his free hand.* MURPHY *quickly grabs* DAVE, *pinning his arms back.*)

JIM: This is another member of the group, Sergeant. Yes, the big fish!

MURPHY: Three in one night! *(To* DAVE*)* Come along, you. The federal authorities are entertaining your two buddies right now. They'll be glad to have you join the little party. *(He hustles* DAVE *off left.* JIM *puts his free arm around* SANDRA.*)*

JIM: This has been quite a night, even without the honeymoon! But, Sandra, you shouldn't have tackled Dave all by yourself.

SANDRA: It was all right, Jim. I told him I had a gun in my purse.

JIM: Oh, no!

SANDRA: After all, you told Professor Stapleton that it almost worked for Alice Palmer, and I was willing to beat them with their own trick. I couldn't let Dave escape.

JIM: I suppose you realized the significance of the identical corsages? *(She nods.)* That finally hit me, too. When I saw Alice Palmer in Murphy's office, wearing the same corsage, I knew it must have come from Dave. Oh, why didn't I think of that sooner?

SANDRA: Well, you had other things on your mind.

JIM *(Suddenly):* Hey, our flight is scheduled to take off any minute! Let's get going, Mrs. Dawson.

SANDRA: Ms. Bennett, if you please!

JIM: All right, Ms. Bennett. But not for long! *(They exit left as curtain falls.)*

THE END

Production Notes

Characters: 5 male; 4 female; offstage voice; male and female extras for Passengers, Airline Personnel and Information Clerks (non-speaking parts). Note: The actresses playing Sandra and Alice should resemble each other.

Playing Time: 40 minutes.

Costumes: Everyday modern dress. Sandra and Alice have identical suits, corsages and handbags. Jim carries a coat over his right arm, to conceal briefcase. Porter wears a dark coat and hat. Sergeant Murphy and airline personnel all wear appropriate uniforms.

Properties: Ticket envelopes, briefcase and handcuffs, rice, pencil, newspaper, fake gun.

Setting: The lobby of International Airport, serving a large city. The ticket counter is up center, and arrival and departure schedules hang on the wall behind it. Up left is the information desk, with a phone on it and a large sign reading INFORMATION. Several telephones are on a counter down right, with large city phone books near them. There are chairs and benches around the lobby. The atmosphere conveyed should be one of constant activity, with passengers and airline personnel hurrying through the terminal.

Lighting: No special effects.

Sound: Public-address announcements giving flight information are ad libbed occasionally during play.

The Final Curtain

Characters

BOB WATSON, *detective, New York Homicide Department*
JEAN, *his wife*
FRANK PENDER, *director of "After the Dawn"*
BESS TRAVERS ⎫
LINN ALLEN ⎪
KIT DRAKE ⎬ *actors in "After the Dawn"*
TOM JEFFERS ⎪
CORA BENNETT ⎭
POP HOGAN, *stage doorman*
USHER
POLICE OFFICER
EXTRAS, *for audience*

TIME: *Evening.*
SETTING: *The drawing room set in "After the Dawn," a Broadway hit.*
BEFORE RISE: *House lights are on.* BOB WATSON *and his wife* JEAN *take their seats in box extreme left. Other seats may be in same box, with* EXTRAS *who ad lib, in low tones, during following dialogue.*
JEAN *(Excitedly):* Bob! Isn't this wonderful?
BOB: These seats set me back a King's ransom. I hope it's good.
JEAN: It will be. We don't get out very often, and this play is the talk of the town. (BOB *glances at program.*)
BOB: I hope you're right.

JEAN: The critics raved about it. *(Points to audience)* It looks like a sell-out.

BOB *(Grinning):* You'd make a great press agent. It's a shame you ever settled down and became an old detective's wife.

JEAN: Well, with Bess Travers as the star of the show, I know I'll love it.

BOB: Yes. You were pretty friendly with her at school.

JEAN *(Nodding):* Yes. I remember her in our drama club plays. It's great that she finally reached the top. (BOB *glances at program again.*)

BOB *(Reading): After the Dawn.* The title doesn't tell much about the play.

JEAN: It's a marvelous show! *(Quickly)* It's one of the latest British stage hits. Bess plays Lady Agatha, a rich woman who's in love with a much younger man. Her husband learns about the young man, and he—(BOB *waves hand.*)

BOB: Hold it right there! If you tell me any more about the plot, I won't have to see the play!

JEAN: John Morris plays Bess's husband. He's *divine.*

BOB *(Sarcastically):* Morris has been *divine* in every Broadway play for twenty-five years. He's a little over the hill, if you ask me.

JEAN *(Heatedly):* No one's asking you. He's still a Broadway idol to most people. By the way, Frank Pender directed this.

BOB: Who?

JEAN: Frank Pender. You must have heard about him. I knew him slightly at school, and he was terribly clever. *(Grinning)* I wonder whether he still likes Bess.

BOB *(Amused):* The plot thickens.

JEAN *(Nodding):* There's more drama backstage than the audience ever dreams of.

BOB: Have you heard from Bess lately, now that she's so important?

JEAN: Yes. I met her after I watched the rehearsal a few weeks ago.

BOB: You mean you've already seen this play?

JEAN *(Slowly):* Yes. . . . I didn't want to tell you, but I really wanted to see it again.

BOB *(Sadly):* And I paid all that dough for these seats.

JEAN: Rehearsal is different. It isn't a finished performance. I want to hear the applause and see the lights, and besides, I told Bess we'd be here tonight. Maybe she'll invite us backstage after the show.

BOB: No, thanks! I'm not cut out for show business. Now, give me a nice case of homicide, and—

JEAN *(Quickly):* Bob, please!

BOB: I guess British dramas and I don't mix very well. *(House lights are dimmed, and a spotlight shines on theater curtain. A dim light may also be cast upon theater box.)*

JEAN: I'm so excited. There's something about curtain time—can't *you* feel it?

BOB *(Quickly):* O.K. O.K. Let me get my money's worth. *(Curtain rises upon drawing room. French doors up center open onto country scene. Closet is up right. Large sofa is down right. Comfortable chairs, tables, writing desk, and lamps complete the setting.* CORA BENNETT, *dressed as Agnes, the maid, arranges flowers at table left.* BESS's *voice is heard calling from offstage.)*

BESS: Agnes! Agnes! (BESS *enters right. She is greeted with applause.* JEAN *rises and applauds enthusiastically.)*

JEAN: Isn't she beautiful? Such a magnificent entrance!

BOB *(Wryly):* I don't think the entrance takes the talents of a Bernhardt. (BESS *crosses stage.)*

BESS: Has Sir Henry arrived home yet?

CORA *(Still arranging flowers):* No, not yet. *(Turns)* But he said he wouldn't be home until late tonight.

BESS: Oh, yes, I recall. *(Pause)* D-Did Godfrey get my message?

CORA: Yes, he called after lunch. I told him that you would expect him later—as usual. *(Shakes head distastefully and continues to arrange flowers)*

BESS *(Quickly):* Godfrey is a friend of the family, nothing more. I know that everyone is telling those wretched stories, but you mustn't believe them.

CORA *(Coolly):* I don't listen to town gossip, ma'am. I only know what I see. *(Regards BESS suspiciously)* Will Mr. Godfrey have dinner with you—on the terrace?

BESS: Why, yes—yes. We'll have dinner together. *(Pause)* I must go out again, Cora. I want to leave a note for Godfrey in case he arrives early. *(Walks to writing desk, sits and begins to write note)*

JEAN: Bess looks terribly pale and tired.

BOB: The Big Time is pretty rough on the nerves.

JEAN: Nonsense! She's lived this role for two months.

BOB: If you aren't quiet, we'll have to watch the play from the sidewalk outside. *(On stage, BESS finishes writing note, places it in envelope, rises, and hands envelope to CORA.)*

BESS: This will explain everything. I—I must go now. *(Glances at window upstage center)* It's going to rain. Will you please get my wrap? (CORA *puts envelope in her apron pocket and walks to closet, upstage right, and opens closet door. Body of man falls from closet.* CORA *screams.* EXTRAS *in audience react and ad lib during following dialogue.* BESS *screams.)* No! John! No! *(Curtain is quickly lowered, and houselights go on.)*

BOB: That was the shortest first act on record. I didn't know *After the Dawn* was a mystery play.

JEAN *(Upset):* It isn't. Oh, Bob, something's wrong!

BOB: What do you mean?

JEAN *(Slowly):* This isn't a murder drama.

BOB *(All attention):* What?

JEAN: That man who fell was John Morris, the male lead in the play.

BOB *(Wryly):* A pretty small part.

JEAN *(Agitatedly):* Bob, listen! He's not supposed to die. I saw the show in rehearsal. There isn't a murder in the first act or any place else.

BOB: Well, maybe they rewrote the opening.

JEAN: Who ever heard of having the hero get killed?

BOB *(Sighing):* Maybe the director thought up some gimmick, and—(USHER *enters box.*)

USHER: Mr. Watson?

BOB: Yes?

USHER: Mr. Pender, the director, would like to see you backstage.

BOB: See *me?*

USHER *(Nodding):* It's very important, sir. Please come with me.

JEAN: I knew something was wrong.

BOB: How did Pender know we were here?

JEAN: I told Bess we had these box seats for tonight's show. Oh, Bob—let's hurry!

USHER *(Pointing left):* There's a flight of stairs that will take us to the left wing. I'll lead the way. (USHER, BOB *and* JEAN *exit.*)

FRANK *(Entering onto apron of stage):* Ladies and gentlemen, we regret to inform you that this evening's performance has been canceled because of the sudden illness of one of the actors.

EXTRAS *(Ad lib):* This is terrible! How dreadful! *(Etc.)*

FRANK: Your money will be refunded at the box office. Watch the papers for announcements of a special performance later. (EXTRAS *start to get up slowly, ad libbing as they do.*) Don't worry—all money will be refunded. *(Aside, to orchestra leader in pit)* Strike up something lively. *(Pause)* No need for alarm, ladies and gentlemen. We regret this incident, but we hope you will return for the special performance of *After the Dawn* at a later date. *(Orchestra music or recorded music plays for a few moments.* EXTRAS *exit.* FRANK *continues aside.)* O.K., they're all out, Jim. Better douse the lights and roll up the curtain. We've asked the whole company to remain on stage. *(Stage curtain rises on set again.* BESS *sits on sofa, crying.* FRANK PENDER *walks over to her.* TOM JEFFERS *and* LINN ALLEN *stand down left.* USHER, BOB, *and* JEAN *enter left.)*

USHER: Mr. Pender, here's Mr. Watson and his wife. (USHER *exits.)*

FRANK *(Shaking* BOB's *hand):* Thanks for coming, Mr. Watson. Bess told me you were in the audience.

BOB: What's all this about?

JEAN: Frank! Bess! What happened?

BESS: It's John Morris.

FRANK *(To* BOB): John Morris, our leading man, is dead. (JEAN *gasps, puts hand over mouth.)* We carried the body to his dressing room, but there was nothing we could do for him.

BOB: Where is the dressing room?

FRANK: I'll show you. (BOB *and* FRANK *exit right.* JEAN *joins* BESS *on sofa.)*

JEAN: What happened, Bess?

BESS: Oh, Jean. It's all so ghastly. I don't know. I can't believe this terrible thing happened. *(Notices* LINN *and* TOM) Please forgive me, Jean. *(Gesturing)* This is Tom Jeffers and Linn Allen—members of the cast. *(Greetings are exchanged.)*

TOM: I guess old Morris rubbed up against the wrong person this time.

LINN: Yes, I'm sorry that this happened to the show—but I'm not sorry for him.

BESS *(Heatedly):* Linn! Tom! You shouldn't talk like that.

LINN: Well, Morris was always making trouble for everyone. I even heard him arguing with *you* after the show last night.

BESS: Why, that's not true!

TOM: Don't be silly, Bess. Everyone knew that Morris was

making things miserable for you. No use trying to protect him now.

BESS: I don't think we should talk about it now.

JEAN *(Putting her hand on* BESS's *shoulder):* Bob and I are here to try to help you. Won't you tell me what it's all about?

BESS: It was really nothing. John complained about my lines in the third act. He said that I played them without feeling.

JEAN: That isn't true! This is your greatest role.

TOM: No one could play Lady Agatha as well as Bess.

LINN: Right, but John wanted her out of the show.

BESS: Don't talk like that. It's not right—not now that this has happened.

JEAN *(To* TOM *and* LINN): When did you last see John Morris alive?

TOM: Not since last night's performance.

LINN: That's the last time I saw him, too.

JEAN: Didn't any of you see him when he arrived for the show tonight?

TOM: No, I didn't know he'd arrived yet.

LINN: You see, John didn't have to appear onstage for twenty minutes after opening curtain. He usually got here just before his entrance. We didn't think anything of it when he hadn't arrived by curtain time.

JEAN: Did you see him, Bess?

BESS *(Quickly):* No! Not tonight. I was too busy getting ready. *(Rises and walks upstage center. Clutches handkerchief nervously)*

TOM: Do you think we can go to our dressing rooms?

JEAN: Yes, but I'm sure Bob will send for you later. (TOM *and* LINN *exit right.* JEAN *goes to* BESS, *takes her arm.)* Bess, I don't think you've told me everything.

BESS: Please, Jean—

JEAN: You never were a convincing liar.

BESS: I'm not lying.

JEAN: Your answer was too pat—too quick. Are you sure you didn't see Morris earlier today?

BESS *(Quickly):* No!

JEAN *(Impatiently):* Come on now, Bess—the truth.

BESS *(Nodding slowly):* Yes, I did see him.

JEAN: What time?

BESS: About four this afternoon. I came to the theater to rehearse a scene in the first act. After rehearsal, I met John, and we went to my dressing room.

JEAN: How long did you stay there?

BESS: I was there for about fifteen minutes. John was still there when I left.

JEAN: Why did he go to your dressing room?

BESS: He wanted to talk about the show. *(Casually)* It wasn't very important. (BOB *enters right, unobserved by women, standing quietly, listening.*)

JEAN: Tom said that Morris wanted you out of the show.

BESS *(Brusquely):* I don't want to talk about that now.

JEAN: The police might ask you the same question.

BESS *(Alarmed):* The police?

BOB *(Kindly, but firmly):* John Morris was poisoned. *(Startled,* BESS *and* JEAN *turn.)* You know I'm a detective with homicide, but I have to call in the captain and the whole team. This is murder.

BESS: Oh, no! That's impossible.

BOB: It's still early to tell what was used, but it looks like cyanide.

BESS: He couldn't have been poisoned! He told me that he was going to stay at the theater this afternoon. . . . And he never ate before a performance. How else could he have been poisoned?

JEAN: He might have taken the poison earlier in the day. You know, a slow-acting kind.

BOB: Cyanide is one of the fastest-acting poisons known.

Morris died shortly after the poison was administered—
and I think he's been dead for some time.

BESS: How can you tell?

BOB: I'll have to get the coroner's report first, but unless I
miss my guess, I think he was poisoned some time late
this afternoon.

BESS: But I was with John this afternoon, and I—
(Suddenly) You don't think that I had anything to do with
this!

JEAN *(Gently):* Bess, you'll have to tell us everything that
happened today.

BESS *(Resigned):* Well, Frank Pender asked Cora and me to
come to the theater to go over the first act.

BOB: Cora?

BESS: Yes, Cora Bennett, the maid in the play. She's in her
dressing room now.

BOB: Why did Frank want to change the first act? This play
has already run for two months.

BESS: Yes, but something bothered Frank. In the opening
of the play now, I get ready to go out shortly after the
curtain goes up. There is a heavy rainstorm, and I return later, but my costume isn't wet. Frank thought that
he could settle the problem by having me wear a coat
over my dress.

BOB: And this was the first performance using the closet
gimmick?

BESS: Yes, the closet was really a prop.

JEAN *(Nodding):* Now that I think of it, I don't remember
seeing Cora get the coat for you in the rehearsal.

BOB: Who else was at the theater this afternoon?

BESS: There were Frank and I, and Kit Drake, my understudy. John came a little later, after the rehearsal had
started.

JEAN: Where were Linn and Tom?

BESS: The closet business didn't involve them, so they

didn't have to be here—although it was Tom who suggested to Frank that I wear a coat.

BOB: Then Tom knew you'd be at rehearsal today?

BESS: Yes, I'm certain that he and Linn knew we were going to be here.

BOB: How long did you rehearse?

BESS: Well over twenty minutes.

BOB: Did you leave the theater with Frank Pender?

BESS: No, Frank had an appointment and left earlier.

BOB: And Cora?

BESS: She left with Frank.

BOB: Then you were alone?

BESS: No. John and Kit were still here.

BOB: Why did you stay?

BESS: As I told Jean, Morris came to my dressing room. It's no secret. (KIT *enters right unobserved by others, and stands listening.*)

BOB: What did Morris want?

BESS *(Coolly):* We discussed the play.

KIT *(Angrily):* Why don't you tell the detective what you really were talking about, Bess? I heard you fighting with him. (*To* BOB) Bess killed him! She wanted him out of the way and she killed him!

BESS *(Shocked):* Kit! What are you saying?

BOB: Is this your understudy? (BESS *nods.*)

KIT *(To* BESS): Why don't you tell the truth? (*To* BOB) I waited outside the dressing room when they were arguing.

BOB: Did you hear what they said?

KIT *(Bitterly):* I heard enough to know that she threatened to kill John Morris. (FRANK PENDER *enters right.*)

FRANK: You don't know what you're talking about.

KIT *(Turning):* You'd like to defend her, wouldn't you? You hated John, too.

BOB *(Calmly):* What did you overhear, Kit?

BESS *(Slowly):* I'd like to answer that. *(Sighing)* Yes, we quarreled. He wanted me to leave the show.

JEAN *(Surprised):* Why? *After the Dawn* is the year's biggest hit.

FRANK *(Quickly):* Morris wanted Kit Drake to play Lady Agatha. She seems to have bewitched him.

KIT *(Angrily):* I was better suited for the role. I should have had it.

BOB *(Holding up his hand):* Quiet, everyone! I'd like to hear Bess's story. *(To* BESS) What happened in your dressing room?

BESS: John told me that if I didn't leave the show, he would do everything to close it. *(More quickly)* Oh, you didn't know John. He was ruthless, cruel. He'd do anything to get his own way.

BOB: How could he close the show?

FRANK: Morris was one of the largest investors in the production.

BESS: Yes, he threatened to withdraw his backing—and to leave the cast, too.

JEAN: And what did you tell him?

BESS: I pleaded with him, but it was no use. I told him it was my first big chance on Broadway. He—he didn't care. He couldn't see anybody but Kit.

JEAN: Why didn't you let him withdraw the money? After all, the play is a hit. Anyone would have quickly bought out his interest.

FRANK: It wasn't that easy. It would take a long time to reorganize, find a new male lead, and countless other details. This was a pretty big production, and we had too much money out to take the chance.

BESS *(Helplessly):* And John wouldn't listen to reason.

KIT *(Quickly);* It was then that you threatened to kill him.

BESS: I told him that I wouldn't let him do anything to

close the show. Yes, I threatened him. I was angry. But I
didn't mean it in the way it sounded.

BOB: How long did Morris stay in your dressing room?

BESS: I don't know. I was terribly upset and left while he
was still there.

BOB (*To* KIT): I suppose Morris left with you.

KIT: No. I listened to the argument in the dressing room,
and then I went home alone.

BOB: And Bess and Morris were still here when you left?

KIT: Yes.

BOB: Was anyone else in the theater when you left?

KIT: No, I didn't see anyone.

BOB: What about ushers? Cleaners? The stage doorman?

KIT (*Shaking her head*): The ushers never get to the theater
before seven. All the cleaning is done in the morning.
And Pop Hogan doesn't report for work until six.

BOB: Pop Hogan?

FRANK: He's the stage doorman. An old-timer in show
business.

JEAN: Yes, I read about him. He was a matinee idol in the
old days.

BOB (*To* BESS): So after Kit left, you were alone with Morris? Now, what time did you leave the dressing room?

BESS: It was five o'clock. I remember looking at my watch
as I left the theater.

BOB (*Slowly*): That would mean John Morris died shortly
after you left. (*Looks at* BESS *steadily*) Or shortly
before.

BESS (*Quickly*): No! John was alive when I left.

BOB: You said that Morris rarely ate before a performance?

FRANK (*Nodding*): I can vouch for that. It was one of his
peculiarities.

BOB: It would be interesting to know how the poison was
administered. Cyanide is quick and fatal.

KIT *(Suddenly):* Why don't you ask Bess about the iced tea she served John in her dressing room?

FRANK *(Angrily):* That's going a little too far.

BOB: Iced tea! You didn't tell us about that.

BESS: I didn't think it was important.

BOB *(Coolly):* It might have been the last thing that Morris drank before his death.

BESS: I always brew myself a hot cup of tea in my dressing room. I have one of those small electric heaters.

JEAN: That's right. We had tea together the day I joined you.

BESS: Before the argument, I offered some to John, but he preferred his iced.

BOB: Did you make it for him?

BESS: No. John has an ice cooler in his dressing room. He went there and got a tray of ice cubes and a glass.

BOB: Did he mix his own drink?

BESS *(Slowly):* Why, yes. I believe he did.

KIT: The tea! The tea was poisoned.

BESS: That's absurd. I drank the tea that was brewed in the same pot. The tea couldn't have been poisoned.

BOB: What about his glass?

BESS: There might have been something in the glass. *(Stops suddenly)* No! I remember now. John went to the sink in my dressing room and rinsed out the glass!

BOB: And after that?

BESS: He poured the tea and added sugar.

BOB: Do you use sugar in your tea?

BESS *(Nodding):* Two lumps.

BOB: Did you use sugar today?

BESS: Yes, the usual amount.

BOB: Where are the tea things now?

BESS: In my dressing room, I suppose. They were there when I left.

KIT: A likely story. You put something in his tea.

BESS: Why would I poison him and leave the evidence there?

BOB: I'll examine them. (LINN *and* TOM *enter right.*)

KIT: I'm not going to stay here.

BOB: I'm afraid no one can leave until the coroner and his team arrive.

KIT: You don't think that I killed John, do you?

BOB: Everyone is a suspect. (*To* TOM) You said you heard Bess and Morris quarreling last night?

TOM: That's true. *(Quickly)* But Bess didn't kill him.

BOB: Where did this argument take place?

TOM: They were talking in the rear wings—near the stage door.

BOB: Did Bess threaten Morris?

TOM: No. She asked him not to close the show.

LINN: Bess wouldn't hurt anyone. Why, she's been wonderful to everyone.

BESS: I can't believe that John is dead. No, I didn't want him to close the show—but *murder!* It's unthinkable!

KIT *(Sneeringly):* You're overacting, "Lady Agatha." (*To* BOB) I'll be in my dressing room. *(Exits)*

JEAN *(Sarcastically):* She's a pleasant sort.

BOB: Bess, we'd like to help you. I'll take a gamble on you, for Jean's sake.

BESS: Then you believe me?

BOB: I'll have to accept someone's testimony if I'm going to get to the bottom of this. (POP HOGAN *enters right.*)

POP: What about the show, Mr. Pender?

FRANK: We'll reopen in a few days, Pop. (JEAN *looks admiringly at* POP.)

JEAN: You're Pop Hogan! I remember my mother telling me about your shows.

POP *(Sadly):* Yes'm. A lot o' things have happened to me since then.

BOB: What time did you get to the theater this evening, Pop?

POP: About six.

BOB: Did any stranger come in after that?

POP: No, sir. Not 'til the regular cast started to arrive.

BOB: And there was no one backstage?

POP: Nope. I punched my time clock, made the early rounds, and went to my post at the stage door.

BOB: You weren't here during the rehearsal this afternoon?

POP: Nope. Didn't know about any rehearsal. A body's got to get some sleep. (*To* FRANK) Is there anything I can do?

FRANK: No, Pop. That's all. (POP *exits right.*)

JEAN: Poor old Pop!

TOM: He was at the top in his day.

LINN: Show business sure is ironic. Why, Pop was the star of the first play in which John Morris played a bit role. It was an old-time melodrama.

BOB: I have to call headquarters.

FRANK: There's a phone in my office. First door to the right. I'll show you. (BOB *and* FRANK *exit.*)

TOM: Come on, Linn. We'd better take off our make-up. (TOM *pats* BESS *on arm.*) Everything will be all right. We believe in you, and your friends will help you.

BESS: You've all been terribly kind. (TOM *and* LINN *exit.*)

JEAN: Cheer up, Bess. I know you're innocent. John Morris must have been horrible to want to spoil your chances on Broadway.

BESS: But I wouldn't kill him. (JEAN *nods.* BOB *enters right.*)

BOB: The squad will be over in a few minutes.

BESS (*Frightened*): What'll they ask me?

BOB: Just tell the truth, and you'll have nothing to worry about.

BESS: But Kit might—

BOB: She'll have to prove the things she said. There are a lot of points that puzzle me, though. How did Morris's body get into the closet?

BESS: I don't know.

BOB: If cyanide was put into the tea in your dressing room, he would have been found there. Our murderer picked a very poor place to conceal the body, since the closet was going to be opened within the first few minutes of the play. That closet was a sure give-away. *(Shakes head)* The tea business is curious, too.

BESS: I told you everything. John poured his own tea. I had some, too.

JEAN: The tea couldn't have been poisoned.

BOB *(Musing):* And Morris used a clean glass. Did anyone else come to your dressing room while Morris was getting the glass and ice?

BESS: No, I was alone.

BOB: How long was he gone?

BESS: No more than a few minutes.

BOB *(Slowly):* Try to remember, Bess. How much iced tea did Morris drink before you left?

BESS: That's hard to say.

BOB: It's very important.

BESS: Well, he might have had half a glass. I can't remember. He drank some, I know.

BOB: Did he leave the glass in your dressing room?

BESS: I don't know. I don't remember seeing it when I got ready for the play tonight.

BOB: Were the other things there?

BESS *(Nodding):* I saw the teapot and tray on my dressing table.

BOB: May I see your dressing room?

BESS: I'll show you the way.

BOB: No, you stay here with Jean. I'll find the way and look around myself. (BOB *exits right.*)

BESS: I don't see how the tea could have been poisoned, since I drank some myself.

JEAN: I think Bob's on to something. *(Suddenly)* Maybe he thinks John killed himself.

BESS: No. If he drank poison in my dressing room, he wouldn't have been found in the stage closet.

JEAN: Yes, that's right. If John died in your room, someone must have moved the body!

BESS: Who would have done that?

JEAN: I think you must have a very good friend in the show.

BESS *(Suddenly):* You don't think it was—Frank?

JEAN *(Thoughtfully):* No. He wouldn't have used the closet.

BESS: That's right. Frank knew about the closet and so did Kit.

JEAN: And Cora was here. (BESS *nods.*)

BESS: The closet was Tom's idea, so of course he knew.

JEAN: What about Linn?

BESS: I'm sure she knew about it, too. Tom tells her everything.

JEAN *(Puzzled):* But that eliminates everyone. Every person in the cast knew that the closet would be used tonight. No one would have used it as a hiding place. (POP HOGAN *enters right.*)

POP: Beg pardon, Miss Travers. The detective fellow would like to see you in your dressing room. It's locked.

BESS: I forgot I locked it. I'll be right there. I have the key. *(To* JEAN*)* Maybe Bob found something.

JEAN: Let's hope so. (BESS *exits right.*)

POP *(Shyly):* I'm glad that you remembered me, ma'am.

JEAN: You were Mother's favorite, Mr. Hogan.

POP: Oh, call me Pop. There aren't many who remember my shows. I guess this is a sad business, but I wouldn't give it up for anything. A lot of people come and go— Great Ones. Take Miss Travers, for instance. She'll be a big name.

JEAN: She is wonderful.

POP: There are a lot of jealous folks in this business, but that's all right. She's got real talent. No one will hurt her.

JEAN: Would anyone want to hurt her, Pop?

POP *(Quickly):* I have to get back to the door. I don't want to lose my job.

JEAN: Please tell me. Why do you think Bess is in danger?

POP *(Smiling faintly):* She's not in danger any more. I reckon no one'll hurt her now.

JEAN: But you can help if you'll tell everything you know. Tom and Linn heard her arguing with John Morris last night.

POP *(Angrily):* Morris was a tyrant! He ruined the stage chances of many good people.

JEAN: Did you know him well? *(Suddenly)* Oh, I remember, he was in one of your plays.

POP *(Slowly):* Yes.

JEAN: After that play, you were forgotten, and *he* became a matinee idol.

POP: Please, ma'am—

JEAN *(Insistently):* Did Morris do something to hurt *your* career? *(Takes* POP's *arm)* Yes, I can see it in your eyes! John Morris was responsible!

POP *(Slowly):* He—he told the producer that I was stealing money from the show. I don't know what happened to the money, but Morris swore that I took it. The producer believed him.

JEAN: Oh, Pop! How dreadful!

POP: After that I played small parts. One-night stands. Fill-ins. John Morris became big time. *(Musing)* Yes, he could hurt a person. He had ways and liked to use them.

JEAN: Did you know that he was planning to ruin Bess's career?

POP *(Nodding):* I heard them fighting last night. I knew Morris would stop at nothing. Nothing! *(Pounds fist in hand)*

JEAN *(Quietly):* You wouldn't let him hurt Bess, would you?

POP: No. And now Morris can never hurt anyone again. (JEAN *steps back.*)

JEAN *(Slowly):* You killed him!

POP: You're crazy! Why, I wasn't even here this afternoon. I was at my boarding house. I've got witnesses.

JEAN: No, Pop. I don't know how you did it, but you killed him, and you put the body in the closet until you could find a better hiding place.

POP: No—

JEAN: Of course! Everyone else knew that the closet would be used tonight, but you weren't at the theater this afternoon. *You didn't know about the closet!* You were the only one who would have hidden Morris there!

POP: Now, look here, ma'am—

JEAN: It was wrong, Pop. You wanted to help Bess—but you were wrong.

POP: You're a pretty smart girl. (JEAN *backs away again.* POP *grasps her wrist.*) Do you think I'd let Morris hurt Bess? She was kind to me. She didn't treat me like an old has-been.

JEAN: You shouldn't have killed him!

POP *(Desperately):* What else could I do? I'm an old man. I couldn't let him ruin her the way he ruined me. *(Pushes* JEAN, *who falls onto sofa.* POP *runs right and hastens down stairs leading to audience.* POP *runs up aisle and disappears.* JEAN *rises.)*

JEAN *(Shouting):* Bob! Bob! (BOB, BESS *and* FRANK *enter right.)*

BOB: Jean! Are you all right?

JEAN: Yes! Yes! *(Points to stairs)* It's Pop! Pop killed John Morris. He went down those stairs. Oh, please go after him!

BOB: Take it easy.

JEAN: But, don't you understand? The killer is getting away.

BOB: He won't go far. When I called headquarters, the chief told me he would put a man at every exit to stop anyone from trying to leave. But you had a narrow escape. You shouldn't play detective.

BESS *(Amazed)*: Pop! I can't believe it!

FRANK: You're in the clear, Bess!

JEAN: I knew that Pop must have hidden the body in the closet because he was the *only* one who didn't know the closet would be used tonight.

BOB: I knew it was Pop, too. And I know how he killed Morris.

JEAN: How? Did you find the tea tray in Bess's dressing room?

BOB: Yes, there was still some tea in the pot, but it wasn't poisoned. Cyanide has an odor similar to bitter almonds, and it would have been easy to detect in the tea.

JEAN: I don't understand. Pop wasn't here this afternoon.

BOB: No, he planned Morris's murder before he left last night.

JEAN: But how? John rinsed the glass before he poured the tea. He used the same sugar bowl as Bess. How could he have been killed?

BOB: That's what stumped me. If Morris had taken the cyanide directly in the iced tea, he would have died before Bess left—but he was still alive. It looked like some sort of delayed action. *(Confusion is heard in rear of theater. POLICE OFFICER escorts handcuffed POP down aisle, up stairs, and onto set.)*

POLICE OFFICER: I found this guy trying to get out the main entrance, Bob.

BOB: Nice work. He's our man, all right.

POLICE OFFICER: I'll take him to headquarters. (BOB *nods.*)

POP: I'm glad Morris is dead.

BOB: I'll be down later to swear out a warrant. (POP *and* POLICE OFFICER *exit.*)

BESS: I feel so sorry for him, in a way. I feel as though I'm to blame.

JEAN: No, Bess. John Morris hurt Pop a long time ago, and he never forgot it. This was Pop's chance for revenge. (*Turns to* BOB) But you still haven't told us how you knew Pop was the killer.

BOB: I knew Pop was guilty when Frank told me that Pop took care of Morris's dressing room. (FRANK *nods.*)

FRANK: Pop always cleaned the dressing room. He looked after John's clothes and tended the ice cooler.

JEAN: I still don't get it. Remember, Bess drank some tea, also.

BOB: Yes, the same tea—the same sugar. There's one thing you forgot. Bess drank *hot* tea.

JEAN: Hot tea? Iced tea? It doesn't make sense.

BOB: There was only one way Morris could have been poisoned. It took time for the cyanide to affect Morris because the ice had to melt!

JEAN: The ice?

BOB: Of course! Pop Hogan mixed cyanide in the ice tray last night. When the cubes melted in Morris's tea this afternoon, well—that was it!

JEAN: That was risky. Anyone might have used those ice cubes.

FRANK: No, I don't think so. No one ever went to Morris's dressing room. It was a pretty safe bet that only he would use the ice cubes.

BOB: Pop didn't realize that Morris would take the ice to Bess's room. When he found Morris's body there while making his rounds tonight, he knew he had to hide the body. I guess you know the rest.

BESS: I don't know how we can ever thank you, Bob.

BOB: Well, you can start by giving a good performance of *After the Dawn.*

BESS: You mean you'll be back?

BOB *(Smiling):* Even if I have to buy another pair of tickets. It will be worth it.

FRANK *(Smiling):* Well, we should be able to get the show back together in a few days, and you'll have the best tickets in the house, compliments of the management. That's the least we can do for you.

JEAN: What about finding a new leading man on such short notice?

FRANK: I'll have a a go at it myself. The role is almost second nature for me now, and it will save breaking in a new actor. Our only problem will be a new understudy for Bess. I doubt if Kit will fit into our company after this.

BESS: Oh, give her a break, Frank. You know how temperamental theater people are.

FRANK *(Hesitating):* If you say so, Bess. But she tried to hurt you.

BESS: She was flattered by John's attention. He turned her head, gave her an exaggerated opinion of herself and her talents. I think she'll straighten out, if we give her another chance.

BOB: I'm glad for your sake that the show won't close.

BESS: You can be sure that Frank and I are going to keep this play at the top.

FRANK: We'd better get the whole company on the stage.

JEAN *(With dramatic gesture):* The show must go on!

THE END

Production Notes

THE FINAL CURTAIN

Characters: 6 male; 5 female; male and female extras for audience members and John Morris.

Playing Time: 30 minutes.

Costumes: Maid's uniform for Cora, police uniform for officer, usher's costume for usher, modern, everyday dress for others.

Properties: Pair of handcuffs, pen.

Setting: A drawing room set of the current Broadway success, *After the Dawn.* Exit to theater wings are right and left. French doors up center open onto pleasant English countryside scene. Closet for wraps is up right. Set is furnished comfortably with chairs, table, writing desk and lamps. There is a large sofa down right. Theater box seats are extreme left, in line with first row of audience aisle if possible. Stage stairs into audience are located either right or left.

Lighting: No special effects.

A Case for Two Detectives

Characters

ANNOUNCER, *male*
SUSAN, *about twenty*
MRS. BARTON, *mother*
MRS. ASHBY, *a weekend guest*
TWO SERVANTS, *male*
MISS MARLOWE, *a secretary*
ANNIE, *a maid*
MR. ALLEN, *a tycoon*
MRS. ALLEN, *his talkative wife*
QUENTIN VAN QUENTIN, *an armchair detective*
RIVETS O'NEILL, *a private eye*

SCENE 1

TIME: *Morning.*
SETTING: *The drawing room in the Barton home on Long Island.*
BEFORE RISE: ANNOUNCER, *a refined man, steps before curtain and nods to audience.*
ANNOUNCER: Ladies and gentlemen, we are going to witness a murder. Rather, we are concerned with the solution of the murder because, when our play begins, the victim has already been "done in." We will not meet him, and it is small loss because I understand he was a bit of a rotter. We are going to present two solutions to the crime: one offered by Quentin Van Quentin, the typical armchair detective; the other given by Rivets

O'Neill, the rough-and-ready private eye. *(Steps to side)* The setting of our play is the palatial Long Island estate of Cyrus Barton. Have you ever noticed that murder mysteries are invariably set on Long Island estates? It seems as though murder is a privilege enjoyed by the rich. Won't you join me in the drawing room? *(Steps forward as curtain rises on drawing room)* Not bad. We wanted something lavish, but this was the best furniture that the props crew could wheedle out of the members of the cast. *(Points to floor, center)* Cyrus Barton was found on that spot. The body has been removed, but the chalk outline shows its position when discovered by Annie, the maid. Annie has an exceptionally strong pair of lungs, and she awakened the household when she stumbled over Barton's remains. *(Calling)* Oh, Annie! (ANNIE *enters left. She curtsies and smiles.*) Won't you scream for us? (ANNIE *gives a blood-curdling shriek. She smiles and curtsies.*) Thank you, Annie. *(She exits.)* But now to get on with the play. I'll be in the left wings should you need me. *(Exits left.* MRS. BARTON *and* SUSAN *enter right.)*

SUSAN *(Nervously):* Oh, Mother, what are we going to do?

MRS. BARTON: It'll be all right, Susan. Cyrus was a dreadful man.

SUSAN: But they'll think that I—

MRS. BARTON *(Firmly):* Don't say it.

SUSAN: But Quentin Van Quentin has started asking questions. He'll soon find out that I wasn't Cyrus's daughter—that I am your child by another marriage.

MRS. BARTON: I should never have invited a famous detective here as a house guest. *(Sighs)* Oh, well—he's a great fourth at bridge. (MRS. ASHBY, *an elderly woman, enters right.*)

MRS. ASHBY *(Agitatedly):* This is terrible. Terrible! Mrs. Barton, I will not stand for this outrage.

MRS. BARTON: I'm sorry, Mrs. Ashby. I wouldn't have invited you had I known that someone was planning to murder Cyrus.

MRS. ASHBY: Murder! And before breakfast, too! I feel like a character in an Agatha Christie novel!

MRS. BARTON: Quentin Van Quentin will be down soon. He'll solve our mystery. *(Commotion is heard offstage.* TWO SERVANTS *enter left, carrying* VAN QUENTIN *in an armchair, which they set at center. They assume stiff pose at either side of chair.)*

MRS. ASHBY: Quentin Van Quentin!

SUSAN: The armchair detective!

MRS. BARTON *(Quickly):* My husband has been murdered and—

MRS. ASHBY: And I haven't had breakfast yet! (QUENTIN *leaps up and waves for silence.)*

QUENTIN: Quiet! *(He focuses attention upon floor, kneels, and takes magnifying glass from pocket. He searches carpet intently with glass.* QUENTIN *pauses, pounces upon object and waves it triumphantly.)* Aha? I found it! I found it!

SUSAN: Do you know the murderer?

MRS. BARTON *(Excitedly):* What have you found?

QUENTIN *(Rising):* My cuff link. I lost it yesterday. *(All sigh with disappointment, as* QUENTIN *returns to armchair, then impatiently dismisses* SERVANTS.*)* Off with you! *(They bow and exit right.* QUENTIN *stares at* MRS. BARTON, *and points his finger at her as he speaks.)* Why did you kill your husband?

MRS. BARTON *(Flustered):* Why—I—I—

QUENTIN *(Interrupting):* Don't deny it. You hated Cyrus Barton. Yesterday, you quarrelled with him. He threatened to cut you out of his will.

MRS. BARTON *(Weakly):* That's not true.

QUENTIN: You met him in this room last night. When he insisted that he was calling his lawyer this morning to change his will, you took a gun and shot him.

MRS. BARTON: But the coroner said that my husband had been poisoned.

QUENTIN: I have no time for petty details. *(All freeze.* AN-NOUNCER *enters left and addresses audience.)*

ANNOUNCER: This part of the play is known as the "Red Herring," or the false clue. All writers use this gimmick to focus suspicion upon an innocent person. I might as well tell you that Mrs. Barton did not murder her husband. The Red Herring is a successful device, because it usually helps an author drag out the play to make it a three-act drama. (ANNOUNCER *exits left.)*

MRS. BARTON *(Tearfully):* But I couldn't have killed my husband. This was his private room. Only he and Annie, our maid, had keys. No one else was ever allowed into this room. When Annie found Cyrus this morning, the door had been locked. She opened it with her key.

QUENTIN: What about the French doors?

MRS. BARTON: They were locked and bolted on the *inside!*

QUENTIN *(Jumping up):* Why doesn't anyone tell me these things? *(Points at* MRS. ASHBY) Mrs. Ashby, why did you kill Cyrus Barton?

MRS. ASHBY *(Indignantly):* This is outrageous!

QUENTIN: Madam, I can always recognize the criminal type! (MRS. ASHBY *looks aghast.* QUENTIN *turns quickly to* MRS. BARTON.) Why did Annie have a key to this room?

MRS. BARTON: To do the dusting and cleaning.

QUENTIN: And he had the only other key?

MRS. BARTON *(Nodding):* Until a week ago. He lost it.

QUENTIN: He lost his key!

MRS. BARTON: Yes, and we never found it. Fortunately, the door was unlocked at the time.

QUENTIN: We're getting nowhere. Locked windows and doors. Men who were poisoned and shot. No clues, no motives! Too strange for fiction! *(He pauses, studies desk rear left.)*

MRS. BARTON: That was my husband's writing desk. (QUENTIN *walks to desk and begins reading papers. He drops pages as he reads. Finally, he clutches one excitedly.*)

QUENTIN: Aha! Cyrus Barton wrote this letter shortly before his death. It bears yesterday's date. (*Everyone gathers around him.*)

MRS. BARTON: What does it say?

QUENTIN (*Reading*): "Dear Sir: I have heard of your intention to marry into my family." (*Looks up and stares at* SUSAN. *He resumes reading.*) "It is my contention that you are a fortune hunter, and there is something you must know. This girl is not my daughter and—" (*He looks at* SUSAN *again.*) The letter ends at this point. He was murdered before he finished. (*To* SUSAN) You'd better tell us everything.

SUSAN (*Hysterically*): I didn't kill him!

QUENTIN: He was exposing you to your fiancé. Whom are you planning to marry

SUSAN: His name is Waldemere. I—I met him at a video arcade. We're both into computers.

QUENTIN: Interesting. And this young man planned to marry you for your money?

SUSAN: No! Waldemere doesn't care about money. He can support me. He runs the computer store downtown.

QUENTIN: Where is he now?

SUSAN: I won't tell you. I won't let you drag him into this.

MRS. BARTON: But my husband knew all about Waldemere. He said in his letter that he heard of Waldemere's intention to marry my daughter.

QUENTIN: Hm-m-m-m. (*Turning sharply; to* SUSAN) Why don't you admit that you killed Cyrus Barton?

SUSAN: But I didn't kill him! If I did, would I leave an incriminating letter on the desk?

QUENTIN: I wish you'd stop asking embarrassing questions. (*To* MRS. BARTON) What did your husband eat for dinner last night? (MRS. BARTON *pauses.*)

MRS. BARTON (*Thoughtfully*): We had a simple meal. Annie, the maid, had been away for two weeks and got back late yesterday afternoon. She fixed something in a hurry. Let me think . . . canned vichyssoise, stuffed pheasant's tongue, and cherries jubilee *à la mode.*

QUENTIN: Nothing unusual there. You say Annie had been away.

MRS. BARTON: Yes. Two weeks' vacation.

QUENTIN: Very interesting. I'm beginning to see the light. (*He walks left and pulls bell cord.*) I must question that young lady.

MRS. BARTON: Surely, you don't think—

QUENTIN: Madam, I wish you'd finish your sentences. It's most distressing. (ANNIE *enters right.*)

ANNIE (*To* MRS. BARTON): You rang, ma'am?

QUENTIN: *I* rang. Now—ah, Annie, I understand that you returned from your vacation yesterday.

ANNIE: Yes, sir. I spent it at Staten Island.

QUENTIN: Elegant, I'm sure. I understand that you have a key to this room?

ANNIE: Yes. I unlocked the door this morning and found Mr. Barton's body. (*Begins to sob*)

QUENTIN (*Holding his hand up*): No dramatics, if you please. (*Sternly*) You're very clever.

ANNIE: Oh, thank you, sir.

QUENTIN: Won't you tell us about the young man you met on your vacation?

ANNIE (*Smiling*): He was ever so nice. He told me that— (*Stops, suddenly*) How did you know about him?

QUENTIN: Elementary. (*Dramatic pause*) Annie, I accuse you of the murder of Cyrus Barton!

MRS. BARTON: Ridiculous!

SUSAN: Not Annie!

ANNIE: I didn't do it!

MRS. BARTON: Why would Annie want to kill Mr. Barton?

QUENTIN: Mr. Barton found out about Annie's young man

at the beach. You see, she posed as Mr. Barton's daughter while on vacation!

MRS. BARTON: Oh, no!

SUSAN: Then he wasn't referring to me in that letter. He was writing to Annie's young man, telling him that she wasn't his daughter.

QUENTIN (Nodding): Annie enjoyed playing the role of a rich man's daughter for two weeks. The young man probably called this house, and Cyrus found out about the deception. He threatened to expose Anne. She decided to kill him while preparing that simple meal last night.

ANNIE: I'm innocent!

QUENTIN (To ANNIE): You served the food. You were the only one who had the opportunity to poison his vichyssoise.

MRS. ASHBY: Poisoned the vichyssoise—how distressing!

QUENTIN (Wryly): Mr. Barton thought so. A little later he came to this room to write that letter to Annie's young man. Annie was impatient. She came here, too. She found him writing the letter.

SUSAN: And she shot him!

MRS. BARTON: But the doors were locked!

QUENTIN: Precisely! It was that clue that told me Annie had killed Cyrus Barton. She wanted to confuse the police. She thought that Mr. Barton had the second key to this room. She didn't know that the key was lost *while she was on vacation!* After killing him, she left the room and locked the doors behind her.

SUSAN: I get it. When you realized that the door had been locked by someone who had the *only* key, you knew that Annie was the murderess.

MRS. BARTON: Ingenious!

QUENTIN (Nodding): The locked room was Annie's downfall. (Walks left and pulls bell cord. 1ST SERVANT enters left. QUENTIN points to ANNIE.) Take her away.

1ST SERVANT: Yes, sir. (*Takes* ANNIE *by arm and starts left with her*)

ANNIE (*Desperately, as they exit*): I didn't do it, I tell you! I didn't do it!

SUSAN (*To* MRS. BARTON): You're free, Mother. Cyrus won't dominate you any more.

MRS. BARTON: And you can marry your young man.

MRS. ASHBY: And I hope now *I* can have my breakfast. (*To* QUENTIN) I'm a little puzzled, though. Couldn't someone have found Cyrus's missing key and murdered him?

QUENTIN: Of course not! While I was searching for my cuff link the morning, I made another discovery. (*Takes key from pocket*) The key was lying on the floor where Cyrus Barton had evidently dropped it.

MRS. BARTON: Incredible! But how did you know about Annie's young man? How did you know that she had told him she was Cyrus's daughter? (ANNOUNCER *enters left.*)

ANNOUNCER: Now, isn't that a silly question? (*Reaches into pocket and withdraws script*) He merely read the last page of the script of this play! (QUENTIN *returns to armchair as* ANNOUNCER *exits left. Curtain*)

*   *   *

SCENE 2

SETTING: *The same as Scene 1.*

BEFORE RISE: ANNOUNCER *steps before curtain and addresses audience.*

ANNOUNCER: We have just seen the armchair detective at work. He wasn't a bad chap, if you don't mind the stuffy type. He will go on solving mysteries until he falls out of his armchair at the age of ninety-two. And now we will meet Rivets O'Neill, Private Eye. The Cloak-and-Dagger-Blood-and-Guts-Bottle-and-Fist-Women-and-Trouble American Detective. His methods are totally different from our armchair detective's, and it will be interesting to see his solution. (ANNOUNCER *exits left, as curtain rises upon drawing room.*)

* * *

AT RISE: SUSAN *stands near French doors, looking into garden. Six quick shots are heard.* SUSAN *screams.* RIVETS O'NEILL *enters center, brandishing a smoking revolver. He is dressed in dark suit, black hat, bright tie and trench coat with turned-up collar. He stares furtively around room, removes handkerchief from pocket and polishes revolver. He places handkerchief and revolver in his pocket.*

SUSAN: Oh, Rivets! How could you? You've shot the chauffeur, the gardner, the gateman, the servant, the stable boy, and the upstairs maid.

RIVETS: A fellow can't be too careful these days. Now, why did you send for me?

SUSAN: Because someone killed my father.

RIVETS: So somebody did the old man out of his Social Security.

SUSAN *(Nodding):* He had been working on an important government project.

RIVETS: Everybody knew about your old man's great inventions. A computerized ketchup dispenser, wasn't it?

SUSAN *(Nodding):* His present work was far more important. He was doing hush-hush, top-secret research.

RIVETS: And you think someone bumped him off because of that work?

SUSAN: Yes. Daddy conducted some experiments in his lab upstairs. He was prepared to turn over his findings to the government today.

RIVETS: Who knew about his work?

SUSAN: His secretary, Miss Marlowe.

RIVETS: Anybody else in the house?

SUSAN: Mother and I. There are servants, of course, and

Mr. and Mrs. Allen. Mr. Allen's a businessman—a friend of Dad's.

RIVETS: What happened to your dad?

SUSAN: We found him in this room this morning. He had been stabbed, shot and poisoned. There was a heavy rope around his neck, too.

RIVETS *(Seriously):* Yeah, it sure sounds like foul play. *(Brightly)* I never had a case I couldn't handle. I'd like to speak to this Marlowe dame.

SUSAN: I told her we'd be down here.

RIVETS: Good! I'll solve this case in no time, and then you and I can be on our way.

SUSAN *(Fluttering):* Oh, Rivets!

RIVETS: I'll take you to the Big City and show you the sights.

SUSAN: Oh, Rivets!

RIVETS: We'll stay at the best places. I'll show you how to live, live, live!

SUSAN: Oh, Rivets!

RIVETS: Take it easy, honey. Your record's stuck. *(Glancing left)* Where's that so-called secretary? (MISS MARLOWE, *an attractive young woman, enters left. She smiles coyly as she sees* RIVETS.)

MISS MARLOWE *(Ingratiatingly):* Mr. O'Neill, I presume.

RIVETS *(Gruffly):* What did you do last night? *(He studies* MISS MARLOWE *for a moment.)* Better still, what are you doing tonight?

MISS MARLOWE: Oh, are you looking for the murderer?

RIVETS: With you around, why should I look for anyone else?

SUSAN: Keep your mind on business.

RIVETS: Oh, I am! *(To* MISS MARLOWE) I understand that Barton finished his work for the government, and was about to send off his findings.

MISS MARLOWE: Yes, a government messenger was due to pick up the papers today.

RIVETS: Where are the papers now?

MISS MARLOWE: In the lab.

RIVETS: Can you check on them?

MISS MARLOWE: Yes, I have the key.

RIVETS: Good! We'll go together. *(He starts left with* MISS MARLOWE. SUSAN *pushes him aside and glares at him frostily.)*

SUSAN *(Coldly):* I'll go with Miss Marlowe. (SUSAN *and* MISS MARLOWE *exit left.)*

RIVETS *(Shrugging):* So, kill a guy for trying! *(He walks around room, steps in front of wall mirror and adjusts tie.* 2ND SERVANT, *wearing mask and carrying gun, enters right.* RIVETS *is unaware of him.* SERVANT *crosses stage until he is a few feet from* RIVETS. *He raises gun and takes careful aim.* RIVETS *spins and grasps* SERVANT'S *arm. Scuffle ensues and gun falls to floor.* RIVETS *and* SERVANT *continue fighting on floor, with loud groans and grunts.* RIVETS *gets up, drags* SERVANT *to his feet, and tears mask off face.)* Who are you?

SERVANT: I'm not talking. (RIVETS *twists* SERVANT'S *arm.)*

RIVETS: I'll snap it off.

SERVANT: No—

RIVETS: Yes.

SERVANT: I'll talk.

RIVETS: Let's hear it, loud and clear. *(He loosens grip on* SERVANT'S *arm.)*

SERVANT: My arm!

RIVETS *(Loudly):* Who are you?

SERVANT: John.

RIVETS: John *who?*

SERVANT: Smith.

RIVETS: Unusual. Who paid you?

SERVANT: I can't tell. (RIVETS *begins to twist* SERVANT'S *arm again.)* Nobody paid me.

RIVETS: You're lying.

SERVANT: No.

RIVETS: Somebody wanted to kill me.

SERVANT: No.

RIVETS: Who's your boss?

SERVANT: Cyrus Barton.

RIVETS: He's dead. You're lying.

SERVANT: No—

RIVETS: Yes!

SERVANT: I don't know who killed him.

RIVETS: Where did you get the gun?

SERVANT: A birthday present from my mother.

RIVETS: Where's your boss's hideout?

SERVANT: I don't know.

RIVETS: Who bumped off Barton?

SERVANT: I don't know.

RIVETS: You're lying!

SERVANT *(Strongly):* No.

RIVETS: Yes.

SERVANT: No!

RIVETS *(Quickly):* No.

SERVANT: Yes!

RIVETS *(Triumphantly):* Ha! I fooled you that time! (ANNOUNCER *quickly steps onto stage from left.)*

ANNOUNCER: I would like the audience to take notice of the short, crisp dialogue. This kind of dialogue flourished during Ernest Hemingway's day. It has traveled a long way since that time. *(Sadly)* I won't say in *which* direction! *(Exits left)*

RIVETS: I'll give you one more chance. Start talking!

SERVANT *(Helplessly):* All right, I'll talk. I saw you coming into the house. I—I had to kill you.

RIVETS: But why? (SERVANT *sighs.)*

SERVANT *(Pointing to* RIVETS's *tie):* I hate that tie! *(He dusts off hands and exits jauntily left.* MR. *and* MRS. ALLEN *enter right.* MRS. ALLEN *is nervous and talkative.)*

MRS. ALLEN *(Clucking):* Who could have done it?

ALLEN: Marsha, don't worry. They'll find the killer. *(To* RIVETS) Who are you?

RIVETS: The question is, who are *you?*

ALLEN *(Pompously):* I am *the* Edgar Allen—financier, tycoon, Wall Street wizard, and suburban commuter. *(Points to* MRS. ALLEN*)* And this *(Swallowing hard)*—is my wife!

MRS. ALLEN *(Gushing):* Poor Cyrus! *(To* RIVETS*)* Young man, do you know who killed him? Of course, his work was top-secret. He never had any time to spend with his poor wife. She never left the house. And she always loved the arts. *(Proudly)* I enjoy the arts, too. Have you read any of Molière's plays? (RIVETS *opens his mouth to speak, but* MRS. ALLEN *rattles on.*) I loved *Les Précieuses Ridicules,* but there are some people who prefer *Le Misanthrope.* Of course, there are others who don't like Molière at all. He's too—too *French,* if you know what I mean. (RIVETS *scratches his chin in bewilderment.*) Well, I suppose one mustn't live in the past, must one? *(To* ALLEN*)* Oh, Edgar, you're so quiet! Haven't you anything to say?

ALLEN *(Sweetly):* Yes, my dear. *(Loudly)* Shut up! (MRS. ALLEN *is taken aback.*)

RIVETS *(To* ALLEN*)*: So—you're a big businessman?

ALLEN: I dabble in the market. In the past few months, I haven't been too busy. Meetings at Du Pont. A merger with General Motors. Small stuff like that.

RIVETS *(Nodding):* Things are tough all over. Were you here last night?

ALLEN: Yes. Barton wanted to confer with me on his project.

RIVETS: You knew about his work?

ALLEN: He trusted me completely. (MISS MARLOWE *and* SUSAN *enter left.*)

MISS MARLOWE *(Excitedly):* The papers—they're gone!

SUSAN: The lab has been ransacked!

RIVETS: Well, now we have a motive for Barton's death.

SUSAN: What can we do?

RIVETS: When we find the papers, we'll have the murderer.

SUSAN: But the killer might have taken the papers and escaped.

RIVETS *(Shaking head):* There weren't any strangers in this house. Barton was robbed and killed by someone he trusted.

MISS MARLOWE: Do you mean that one of *us* killed him?

RIVETS *(Dramatically):* Fact is, lady, the murderer is in this room! *(He pulls revolver from pocket and tugs at* ALLEN'S *wig, which comes off. Papers fall out of wig, onto floor.)* Here's the killer! Allen, you killed Barton and hid the secret papers under your wig!

MRS. ALLEN *(Tearfully):* Oh, Edgar! *(Points to wig)* And I thought your hair was naturally curly!

RIVETS *(To* ALLEN): I knew that you killed Barton when I heard that he had been stabbed, strangled, shot and poisoned. You're a successful businessman. You wouldn't leave anything to chance. He caught you stealing his secret research papers, so you killed him!

SUSAN: But Mr. Rivets, how did you know he had hidden the papers under his wig? (ANNOUNCER *enters left.)*

ANNOUNCER *(Pointing to* RIVETS): He read the script, too! (ANNOUNCER *exits.)*

RIVETS *(To* ALLEN): Now, you're going to die! *(He fires revolver and* ALLEN *falls to floor.)*

MISS MARLOWE: You killed him! You fiend! *(She lunges at* RIVETS, *but he sidesteps and levels revolver at her.)*

RIVETS: You were Allen's accomplice. He couldn't get into the lab without *your* key.

MISS MARLOWE: Yes, I helped him!

RIVETS: Why did he want the plans?

MISS MARLOWE: Mr. Barton's plans would have been worth a fortune. Allen knew how to turn them into gold, and now you've killed him! *(She laughs shrilly.)* But you haven't won. Allen and I wired a bomb to explode in exactly *one minute*! *(She glances at wristwatch.)* You can't escape!

SUSAN *(Frantically):* What can we do?

MISS MARLOWE: You have thirty seconds!

RIVETS: Where is the bomb?

MISS MARLOWE: You'll never find it. *(Glances at watch)* Twenty seconds!

MRS. ALLEN *(Indignantly):* This isn't good for my nerves. Loud noises frighten me. And my first editions will be ruined! *(To* RIVETS*)* Are you a collector . . .?

RIVETS *(Sharply):* Shut up!

MISS MARLOWE: Ten seconds!

SUSAN: Goodbye, Rivets.

RIVETS: Goodbye—

MISS MARLOWE *(Studying watch):* Five seconds—four—three—two—one! (MRS. ALLEN, RIVETS *and* SUSAN *steel themselves for explosion. A faint "pop" is heard offstage.* AN-NOUNCER *enters left. He bows rather apologetically.)*

ANNOUNCER: We had planned to introduce a deafening explosion at this point, but our plans went wrong. *(Shakes head sadly)* Our sound-effects person is a real amateur! *(He exits.)*

RIVETS *(To* MISS MARLOWE*)*: And this is for you, sister! *(Points gun at her and fires. She falls to floor. He turns to* SUSAN.*)* Well, I cleared up this case.

MRS. ALLEN *(Sighing):* Thank heavens that's over. It reminded me of one of those thrilling mystery stories. Do you like mysteries? (RIVETS *levels gun at her.*) Really, I think mystery writers are quite ingenious. Of course, their stories are always filled with doddering old ladies and retired colonels, but one can't have everything. And another thing—(RIVETS *fires gun.* MRS. ALLEN *falls to floor.)*

RIVETS *(To* SUSAN*)*: Let's get out of here. *(Points to "bodies")* This place is getting crowded. *(He and* SUSAN *step across bodies and exit. Curtain falls.* ANNOUNCER *enters left and addresses audience.)*

ANNOUNCER: I hope you have enjoyed *A Case for Two Detec-*

tives. Their methods were different, but each sleuth came up with a surprising solution. There's one thing, though. Both detectives were WRONG! *(Pause)* Who killed Cyrus Barton? *(Shakes head sadly at audience)* Why, the *butler,* of course! Didn't you know that the *butler* is always the murderer? And who is the butler? Well, I'll tell you—

MRS. BARTON *(Calling from offstage):* Jarvis! Jarvis!

ANNOUNCER *(Taking small tray from inside suit jacket, cup and saucer from jacket pocket, and placing them on tray; pompously):* Coming, madam! *(Strikes a stiff pose, throws back shoulders and exits with a solemn step, carrying tray.)*

THE END

Production Notes

A CASE FOR TWO DETECTIVES

Characters: 6 male; 6 female.

Playing Time: 30 minutes.

Costumes: Modern everyday dress. Annie and Servants wear appropriate uniforms. 2nd Servant later puts on black mask. Mr. Allen wears wig. Rivets wears black hat, dark suit with handkerchief in pocket, bright necktie and trench coat with turned-up collar. Miss Marlowe wears watch. Announcer wears tuxedo, and in final scene carries small tray, cup and saucer in jacket pocket.

Properties: Guns, magnifying glass, cuff link, key, papers, letter, script, armchair.

Setting: The drawing room of the Bartons' Long Island home. French doors leading to garden are up center. Desk is nearby. Other entrances are right and left. Mirror hangs on wall right. Chairs, tables, lamps, etc., complete setting.

Lighting: No special effects.

Sound: Gunshots, offstage "pop," as indicated in text.

An International Affair

Characters

FRAN, *a reporter*
TOD HUNTER, *director of art gallery*
GRETEL BECK, *a friend of Fran's*
VAN LOON, *a visitor to the art gallery*
Ms. SPENCER, *Tod's secretary*
WESTERN UNION MESSENGER
GUARD
SPECTATORS, *male and female*

TIME: *Late afternoon.*
SETTING: *The International Exhibition in a New York art gallery. Desk, with telephone and papers on it, is down right. Table holding small statue and objet d'art is at left. Statue should be mounted higher than other pieces so that it is in view of audience. Paintings, crafts, etc., adorn walls.*
AT RISE: Ms. SPENCER *is writing at desk.* SPECTATORS *are milling about, studying exhibits. Chime is heard offstage, and* GUARD *enters left.*
GUARD (*Announcing*): Four o'clock. The gallery is closing now. Will everyone please leave? (SPECTATORS *slowly move right and left and exit.* GUARD *joins* Ms. SPENCER *at desk.*) Well, the new boss had a pretty good set-up.
Ms. SPENCER: Yes, Mr. Hunter's International Exhibition has been a big success.
GUARD: It's about time this gallery made it. I'm glad for

Hunter, though. He's worked hard since he came a few weeks ago.

Ms. SPENCER: It's a shame that this exhibit can't stay longer. I'm sorry these works of art have to be returned tonight.

GUARD: Don't worry—he'll come up with something good for the next show. That young man has brains. *(Exits right. GRETEL and FRAN enter left.)*

GRETEL *(Excitedly):* Has Mr. Hunter come back yet?

Ms. SPENCER: No, Gretel, but he said you were to stay here until he got back.

FRAN *(To GRETEL):* Stop worrying, Gretel! Everything will be all right.

GRETEL: I tried to tell myself that, but I am worried, with Dad leaving in such a rush yesterday when he got the phone call from the hospital in Amsterdam about Mother's illness. He was upset, too.

FRAN *(Nodding):* I imagine he must have been terribly worried.

Ms. SPENCER *(To GRETEL):* Have you heard from your father since he returned to Amsterdam?

GRETEL: Not a word. He should have called me by now.

Ms. SPENCER: You'll probably hear tonight.

GRETEL: I hope so.

FRAN: Let's take one more look at the pictures while you wait for Mr. Hunter. Ms. Spencer wants to get her work done.

Ms. SPENCER: That's a good idea. I don't think Mr. Hunter should be too much longer. (FRAN *and* GRETEL *walk left and admire objects on table.)*

FRAN: That's a lovely statue your dad designed for First Prize for the International Artist Award. I wouldn't mind having it for my mantelpiece.

GRETEL: They're going to present it to the winner in Amsterdam.

FRAN: I wonder who will deliver it to Amsterdam, since your dad had to go there so suddenly, before this exhibition closed. And the judges still have to meet.

GRETEL: I don't know. Mr. Hunter will have to find someone. I can't take time off from my studies now, unless it's absolutely essential.

FRAN *(Warmly):* Well, don't worry. Tod will make all the arrangements. He can take care of anything.

GRETEL: You're fond of him, aren't you?

FRAN *(Laughing):* How do you know?

GRETEL *(Smiling):* That's easy!

FRAN *(Sighing):* I wish it were easy for him to see it. *(Dreamily)* I fell for him the first time I met him.

GRETEL: How did you meet him?

FRAN: I covered a couple of his exhibits at the gallery he used to be with.

GRETEL: He's very nice. I hope he'll like it here. (TOD HUNTER *enters right.)*

TOD: Hello, Ms. Spencer. Were there any calls for me?

MS. SPENCER: No, Mr. Hunter.

TOD *(To* GRETEL *and* FRAN): Hello, Fran, Gretel. Sorry to have kept you waiting.

FRAN *(Lightly):* Oh, think nothing of it. Reporters are used to waiting for stories and interviews.

TOD: Any word from your dad, Gretel?

GRETEL: No. I tried calling him at our house in Amsterdam, but there was no answer. He said he'd call me, but I haven't heard from him yet.

TOD *(Shaking head):* I'm sorry. I hope there's nothing seriously wrong with your mother. *(To* MS. SPENCER) I'm expecting a call from the insurance company about the attempted robbery here last week.

FRAN: What's that?

TOD: There's no story there, Fran. It didn't amount to much. Someone tried to force the rear door but didn't get in. He must have been scared off by security making rounds.

FRAN: Tod! Do you mean to tell me you had a newspaper story and you didn't let me know?

TOD *(Laughing):* Hardly a front-page story! Nothing was missing. I'll be sure to let you in on the next story, though. *(Phone rings.)*

Ms. SPENCER *(Into phone):* Mr. Hunter's office. . . . Yes, yes. . . . Downstairs? One moment. *(To* HUNTER) Mr. Hunter, there's a Mr. Van Loon in the lobby who wants to see you.

TOD: Have him come up.

Ms. SPENCER *(Into phone):* Send him up, please. *(Hangs up)*

GRETEL: Van Loon? Why, he's Dad's agent. He arranged exhibitions of Dad's here, with Mr. Preston—the former gallery director.

TOD: I'll be glad to meet him. Now that Preston has left, I'll have a lot of business with him.

GRETEL: I haven't seen Mr. Van Loon in years. I didn't even know he was in America.

TOD *(To* Ms. SPENCER): I guess you can call it a day. *(She finishes sorting papers and rises.)*

Ms. SPENCER: Good night, everyone. *(Exits left.* VAN LOON *enters right, crosses to* TOD, *extends hand.)*

VAN LOON: Mr. Hunter, my name is Van Loon. *(They shake hands.* VAN LOON *suddenly recognizes* GRETEL.) Why, Gretel Beck! I almost didn't recognize you.

GRETEL: It's been a long time, Mr. Van Loon.

VAN LOON: You were a small girl when I last saw you in Holland. It was your father who asked me to come here.

GRETEL *(Excitedly):* You spoke to Father?

VAN LOON: Yes, he called at my hotel here yesterday, before his plane left for Amsterdam. It was about the statue.

TOD: The statue?

VAN LOON *(Nodding):* He knew I was planning to fly back to

Holland tonight, so he asked me to return the statue to Amsterdam in time for the award presentation next week.

GRETEL: How did he know you were in New York?

VAN LOON *(Quickly):* Oh, we'd been in touch earlier. *(Walks to table and picks up statue with right hand)* This must be it. A lovely work!

GRETEL: Well, Father has made more valuable pieces, but this one has been popular during the exhibition. (VAN LOON *replaces statue, extracts handkerchief from pocket with right hand and wipes brow, then returns it to pocket.)*

TOD: I wish Mr. Beck had told me to expect you to call for the statue. *(Uneasily)* It's highly irregular to—

VAN LOON *(Quickly):* He left very hurriedly, as you know. He told me he'd meant to call you but there was so little time to make the plane. *(Starts to reach into jacket pocket)* If you wish to see my credentials—

TOD: Oh, I guess that Gretel can vouch for you.

GRETEL *(Slowly):* Yes, Mr. Van Loon's worked with my father for a long time.

FRAN: Mr. Van Loon, can you tell me something about the statue? I'm from the *Globe* and I'd like to put this story on the front page.

VAN LOON: Well, Mr. Beck's work has always attracted wide attention. He was asked to make this statue for the annual International Artist Award.

TOD: I was pretty lucky to get it for my International Artist Exhibition.

FRAN *(To* VAN LOON): Are you a sculptor, too?

VAN LOON *(Smiling):* Well, I try, but I will never reach the heights of Beck.

GRETEL: Oh, you worked with my father many times.

VAN LOON: In a way, I help with designs. I worked on the design for this one, too.

FRAN: Well, you should be able to give me some good background material for a story.

VAN LOON *(Shortly):* Some other time. I'm rather anxious to return to the hotel and finish packing. My flight has been canceled, and I'm leaving for Canada, to pick up another flight to Amsterdam there.

TOD: If you'll come to my office, we can take care of the release forms.

VAN LOON *(Relieved):* Of course, of course. *(To* GRETEL*)* I'll see you before I leave, Gretel. *(*TOD *and* VAN LOON *exit right.)*

FRAN *(Sighing):* It doesn't look as though I'll get a story after all.

GRETEL: He doesn't act like Mr. Van Loon, as I remember him. Of course I haven't seen him in ages, but he seems so different. *(Walks to table)* And there was something else, too.

FRAN *(Suddenly alert):* What's the matter, Gretel?

GRETEL: I guess I'm just upset about my father, but— *(Suddenly)* Yes, I knew something was wrong! *(Excitedly)* He picked up the statue with his *right* hand.

FRAN: I don't think he could have managed too well with his teeth.

GRETEL: Please be serious. I've seen Van Loon work with my father. He's *left-handed!* He never used his right hand! Father always remarked about it.

FRAN: But, it's been so many years.

GRETEL *(Shaking head):* No, I'm sure I'm right. Why, this man even used his handkerchief with his right hand! I remember Van Loon used to joke about his right hand being practically useless.

FRAN *(Puzzled):* But what could it mean?

GRETEL: I don't know, but I'm sure that man isn't the real Mr. Van Loon!

FRAN: But you did recognize him, didn't you?

GRETEL: Yes, I thought I did at first, but—

FRAN: And he certainly acted as though he knew you.

GRETEL: If someone's posing as the real Van Loon, he'd

find out as much as possible about Dad and me ahead of time!

FRAN: You have to be sure before you make any accusations.

GRETEL *(Uneasily):* I just don't trust him.

FRAN: But why should anyone want to pose as Van Loon?

GRETEL *(Quickly):* He wants the statue! Didn't you notice how anxious he was to get it and leave?

FRAN: The statue is a nice work, but it isn't really valuable. Why should he want to steal it?

GRETEL *(Suddenly):* I don't know, but we mustn't let this man have the statue. Oh, Fran. You have to figure out a way to speak to Tod before he gives the man the statue!

FRAN: He won't believe me. He'll just think I'm telling him this to get a story for the paper.

GRETEL: We'll have to do something.

FRAN: We have to figure out why that man is impersonating Van Loon.

GRETEL: It must be the statue. That's the only thing that interested him.

FRAN: I still don't get it. If he wanted the statue, why wouldn't he have stolen it before?

GRETEL: Maybe he didn't have the opportunity. Ms. Spencer is at the desk all day. And the guards are on duty at the entrance of the building. *(Snaps her fingers)* Someone did try to break in last week!

FRAN *(Thoughtfully):* That's right, and the statue's been on exhibit here for a week. I think you're right! I'd better get Tod in here somehow. Keep an eye on the statue. *(Exits right. GUARD enters right with WESTERN UNION MESSENGER.)*

GUARD: A message for you, Miss Beck.

MESSENGER: A telegram, miss. *(GRETEL quickly signs for message. MESSENGER and GUARD exit right. GRETEL reads message and stares at it for a while, then sits at desk. TOD and FRAN enter right.)*

Tod: I don't know what kind of nonsense you're telling me, but you'd better be right.

Fran: Wait until you hear Gretel's story. *(They cross to desk.)* Why, Gretel, what's the matter?

Gretel: I don't know. *(Hands cable to* Tod*)* It's from Father.

Tod *(Reading):* "Arrived Holland 10:00 A.M. Mother well. All a mistake. She did not have anyone call me to return. Love, Father." *(Places paper on desk)* That's pretty strange.

Gretel: Someone wanted Father out of the country.

Fran: Don't you see, Tod? Gretel's dad would have known right away that the man in your office is not Van Loon.

Gretel *(Quickly):* And someone called Father so that he'd be sure to go to Amsterdam immediately.

Tod: The man has Van Loon's credentials. I saw them.

Gretel: They could have been forged—or stolen. Tod, you have to call the police!

Tod *(Helplessly):* I can't do that. I'll admit that something's not right, but I haven't any proof against the man.

Fran: Well, I hope you're not going to give him the statue.

Tod: No, I'll tell him that I can't release the statue without Beck's written permission. Wait here. I'm going to get our mysterious visitor. *(*Tod *exits right.)*

Gretel *(Nervously):* I'm afraid!

Fran: Leave everything to Tod. Don't worry.

Gretel: But what about the real Van Loon? If that man has his credentials, there's no telling what might have happened to Dad's friend.

Fran: It's a good thing you remembered that Van Loon was left-handed.

Gretel: That wasn't hard. I watched Mr. Van Loon work with Dad many times. *(Looks at statue left, as* Tod *and* Guard *enter right quickly)*

Tod *(Hurriedly):* Check all the rooms. *(To* Guard*)* And call downstairs and tell the security guard that no one should leave the building.

Guard: Yes, sir! *(Exits left)*

FRAN: What happened?

TOD: He's gone! He's not in my office!

FRAN: He must have suspected that something went wrong.

GRETEL: We have to find him! He has to tell us what happened to the real Van Loon.

TOD: He won't get out. The main entrance will be locked.

FRAN *(Shivering):* Yes, but that means we're in here with that character. I don't like it.

TOD: You'll be O.K. (GUARD *enters left.*)

GUARD: Everyone's been alerted, Mr. Hunter.

TOD: Good! Was it you who brought him up here?.

GUARD: Yes, sir. We stopped at the booth in the main entrance first. He wanted to leave his suitcase there.

FRAN: A suitcase?

GUARD *(Nodding):* Yes. A small, black bag.

TOD: Get it for me right away! (GUARD *exits right.*) Well, it certainly seems as though our friend almost fooled us. *(Phone rings.* TOD *answers. Into phone)* Yes—what? Send him right up! *(Hangs up phone and stands perplexed)* Now, this is interesting! That was security at the main entrance. They say there's a man downstairs who wants to see me.

GRETEL: Who is he?

TOD: The man said his name is—Van Loon!

FRAN: What?

GRETEL: Mr. Van Loon!

FRAN *(Quickly):* Let me at that phone. I want to call my paper!

TOD: Hold it! Let's see this man first. (VAN LOON *enters right. He is now wearing a different suit and carries an overcoat.*)

VAN LOON: You are Mr. Hunter, I presume?

TOD: Yes, sir! It seems as though we have already met!

VAN LOON: I think that's quite impossible. This is my first visit to the gallery in several weeks.

GRETEL *(Breaking in and going over to him):* Mr. Van Loon, don't you remember me?

VAN LOON: Gretel Beck! This is a pleasure! How is your father?

GRETEL: Didn't he call you yesterday?

VAN LOON: Why, no. I haven't heard from him since I helped work on his last statue.

FRAN *(Suddenly):* Have you lost your wallet or any important papers lately? (VAN LOON *regards her strangely.*)

VAN LOON: No, miss. *(To* TOD) I'm afraid that I'm puzzled.

TOD: Well, someone is in the gallery now—posing as you!

VAN LOON *(Upset):* But why?

TOD: That's what we have to find out. (VAN LOON *looks at table.*)

VAN LOON: Ah, Mr. Beck's statue is still here, I see.

TOD: Yes. That's what the impostor wanted. Is there anything particularly valuable about the statue?

VAN LOON: The prize-winner will be proud to receive it. But it has little monetary value. It's a simple bronze piece.

TOD: Well, it seems to be pretty valuable to someone.

VAN LOON: Perhaps Mr. Preston could tell you something about that.

TOD: You mean the previous director of this gallery?

VAN LOON: Yes. He displayed all of Mr. Beck's works. I believe it was he who originally insisted on including this statue in the exhibition.

TOD: That's right. The trustees at the gallery dismissed him rather suddenly, and I was named in his place. I finished the plans for the exhibition.

VAN LOON: It is a pity that Mr. Beck isn't here.

FRAN *(Slowly):* Yes, he could have helped us a lot. (GUARD *enters right.*)

GUARD: The black bag's gone from the booth, Mr. Hunter.

TOD *(Determined):* That man must be found.

GUARD: All the offices and galleries have been searched. He's not anywhere!

TOD: That's impossible! Keep looking.

GUARD: Yes, sir. *(Exits)*

VAN LOON: What are you going to do with the statue?

TOD: I'm going to try calling Mr. Beck.

VAN LOON: If I can be of any service, I'll be glad to take it to Amsterdam with me. I am leaving this evening. (TOD *nods.*) Yes, my first flight was canceled an hour ago. Most annoying, indeed!

FRAN: Your flight was canceled?

VAN LOON: Yes, I received word at my hotel a little while ago. *(Looks at statue)* But I don't feel that the statue should be left unguarded.

GRETEL: That's right. We're not sure that the impostor has really left the building. (VAN LOON *picks up statue with left hand.*)

VAN LOON *(To* TOD): I think it will be safer locked in your office.

TOD: Yes, come along with me. (TOD *and* VAN LOON, *carrying statue, exit right.*)

GRETEL *(Relieved):* Well, I feel safe now.

FRAN *(Slowly):* I'm not so sure.

GETEL: You don't distrust this Mr. Van Loon, do you? Why, my family has known him for ages.

FRAN: Yes, and I realize he knows a lot about your father's work. . . . I may be wrong, but—(TOD *enters right.*)

TOD: Mr. Van Loon would like to see both of you in my office.

FRAN: Maybe I'll get a good story, after all. *(Suddenly)* Where's the statue?

TOD: In my office with Van Loon. He—*(Loud commotion is heard offstage.* VAN LOON *enters right quickly. His clothes are disheveled, and he no longer carries his overcoat.)*

GRETEL: Mr. Van Loon! What happened?

VAN LOON *(Quickly):* The statue! He's taken the statue. Someone must have been hiding in the alcove outside Mr. Hunter's office. He attacked me from behind as I was about to enter. He grabbed the statue, and when I turned around—it was like looking into my own face!

TOD: Everyone stay here. I'm sending for the police.

FRAN: Wait, Tod! I have an idea.

TOD: I don't have any time now.

FRAN: Please leave this to me. It's a long shot, I know, but it might pay off. *(Exits right)*

TOD *(Calling):* Fran! Fran! Oh, she's gone. She shouldn't be roaming around alone. I'd better go after her. *(Exits)*

GRETEL: I'll go, too. *(Turning)* Are you all right, Mr. Van Loon? (VAN LOON *sits.*)

VAN LOON: Yes, I'll be all right, after a little rest. Go—find that young woman. (GRETEL *exits right.* VAN LOON *rises and walks to table. He touches empty place where statue stood, and he nods and smiles. Footsteps and sharp commands are heard from offstage.* VAN LOON *glances right and sits down quickly again.* FRAN, *carrying statue, enters right.*)

FRAN *(Excitedly):* I found it, Tod! I found it! *(Sees* VAN LOON) Where's Mr. Hunter? *(At sight of statue,* VAN LOON *rises hurriedly.*)

VAN LOON: Where did you find—that?

FRAN: Where you left it! It was in the inner lining of your overcoat.

VAN LOON: My overcoat?

FRAN: Yes—*your* coat! You said you were attacked outside the office. How did your coat and the statue get inside?

VAN LOON: I don't know what you mean.

FRAN: I noticed that when you stumbled up here with that story about being attacked, you didn't have your coat over your arm. I thought that if I found the coat, I'd have a pretty good chance of finding the statue, too!

VAN LOON: Nonsense! Why, it must have been the impostor who attacked me and then took my coat. You saw him yourself—

FRAN: No—we saw what you wanted us to see. There was no impostor! *You* were the man who came here the first time. You disappeared and returned as the *real* Van Loon!

VAN LOON: I won't listen to this.

FRAN *(Abruptly):* Oh, it was clever. What could have been better than to have us believe that a man posing as you had really taken the statue? You would have been in the clear. No one would have suspected that you posed as— *yourself!*

VAN LOON *(Smiling):* Can you prove that?

FRAN: Yes, I think I can. You knew that Gretel was at the gallery to help with the arrangements for the return of the statue, and you wanted her to be the first person to think that you were an impostor, *not* Van Loon. You purposely handled the statue with your right hand and used your handkerchief with your right hand to make her suspicious.

VAN LOON: I am enjoying your fantastic story.

FRAN *(Quickly):* After Tod left you in his office the first time, you had a wonderful chance to do your "disappearing act." You took the black bag at the guard's booth, left the building with the gallery visitors, and changed clothes in a nearby room. Then you returned as the real Van Loon to steal the statue. Everyone was looking for an impostor!

VAN LOON *(Somewhat menacingly):* What about your proof?

FRAN: You told us too much the first time. You said you were leaving for Canada in less than two hours because of the cancellation of your flight. Now, an impostor might have known your plans and habits pretty well, but he could not have possibly known about the plane cancellation! Only you could have had that information.

VAN LOON: I don't think that's very convincing evidence.

FRAN: That left-handed business puzzled me, too. I'm sure that an impostor would have used his left hand imitating you. He couldn't have overlooked such an obvious characteristic—unless he wanted us to know that he was an impostor!

VAN LOON: I'm going to call Mr. Hunter. Perhaps he can convince you that you are mistaken.

FRAN *(Ignoring the interruption):* And you made another slip, too. When you appeared the second time, you said that you had not spoken to Mr. Beck in weeks, but at the same time, you mentioned that it was a shame he was recalled to Holland. How did you know that? You knew—because you had an accomplice call him and say that his wife was ill. You realized that he would have recognized you immediately, so you had to get him out of the way. (VAN LOON *steps closer and points to statue.)*

VAN LOON: Why should I have gone to such extremes to steal the statue? It has no real value. (FRAN *bangs statue firmly on desk and removes base.)*

FRAN: This is the reason. It is important because of these semiconductor chips. *(Extracts packet from base, opens it and pours chips onto desk)* This statue was used to smuggle computer technology out of the United States. You probably used Mr. Beck's other works, too, and Preston, the former gallery director, sold them. Preston was dismissed suddenly, but this statue was already on its way to the gallery with the chips hidden in the base. That's why you wanted it. (VAN LOON *lunges for packet, but* FRAN *pushes him away.)*

VAN LOON: Give them to me!

FRAN: No! You made the bases for all Mr. Beck's statues. You've been smuggling chips in them for quite some time now. (VAN LOON *suddenly grabs* FRAN'S *arm.)*

VAN LOON: You're much too clever. I'm going to make sure

that no one else hears your interesting little tale. (*Reaches into pocket;* TOD, GRETEL *and* GUARD *enter quickly right.*)

TOD: Someone has already heard the story—and it makes sense to me. The police are on their way. (GUARD *grabs* VAN LOON, *and they exit right.*)

FRAN *(Accusingly):* You were out there all that time, and you didn't help me?

TOD: A confession is pretty good proof. I wanted to catch him in his own trap. Imagine! A man imitating himself!

GRETEL: Yes, he had an iron clad alibi. *(Sadly)* Poor Father. He'll feel terrible when he hears this!

TOD: People will do strange things for money, Gretel. Van Loon placed that above your father's friendship. And it's lucky for us that he wasn't successful when he tried to break into the gallery last week.

FRAN *(Nodding):* That's why he had to come up with this plan.

GRETEL: Fran, you really saved the day.

TOD: Yes, Fran. The gallery could have had a tremendous loss if it weren't for your quick wits—and courage. Preston was in on the whole scheme. He and Van Loon probably thought they had everyone fooled. And they almost got away with it.

FRAN: Never mind Van Loon and Preston. Where's my reward?

TOD: Will you settle for a dinner date—till I ask the trustees for something more tangible?

FRAN *(Smiling):* Dinner will be a good place to start! *(Quick curtain)*

THE END

Production Notes

Characters: 4 males; 3 females; as many male and female extras as desired.

Playing Time: 25 minutes.

Costumes: Modern, everyday dress. Van Loon wears a different suit when he appears the second time. Also, he carries an overcoat the second time. Uniforms for Guard and Western Union Messenger.

Properties: Small statue with removable base, handkerchief, pencil, pad, Western Union envelope and message, papers, packet containing "chips."

Setting: The International Exhibition in a New York art gallery. Entrances are right and left. Desk is down right. A telephone and papers are on desk. Table holding small statue and objet d'art is at left. The statue should be mounted higher than the other articles so that it is in view of the audience. Paintings, handicrafts, and flags of various nations adorn walls. Chairs, tables, and other comfortable furnishings comprise set.

Lighting: No special effects.